A NEW IRELAND

A NEW UNION: A NEW SOCIETY
IRELAND 2030

A TEN YEAR PLAN

Post Brexit Edition

By Paul Gosling

2

Self published in 2020 by:
Paul Gosling
www.paulgosling.net

2nd Edition 2020

ISBN: 978-1-5272-6235-5

Interior and Cover Design
by Mary Campbell
Printed by W&G Baird

***Paul Gosling* is a financial journalist and economic commentator based in Northern Ireland**

A NEW UNION: A NEW SOCIETY

IRELAND 2030

CONTENTS:

FOREWORD

THIS SECOND edition of 'A New Ireland' has been written in response to the unexpected impact of the first edition. But it is also published because in the space of a little more than a year; the context and political conversation around the prospect of Irish unity has move on significantly.

Let us consider some of the changes in the last two years. Brexit has evolved and the UK has left the EU. One result of that is that Northern Ireland will become economically semi-detached from Great Britain, with a border in the Irish Sea. Instead, Northern Ireland will become more closely linked economically to the Republic of Ireland. Increasingly trade in Northern Ireland will be conducted through the euro.

With that closer economic linkage comes a new responsibility on the Republic of Ireland to assist the economic development of the north. Indeed, it seems likely that comments by former Taoiseach Leo Varadkar promising support for capital investment in Northern Ireland is at least partly influenced by the prospect of eventual reunification – and the need to repair NI's economic and fiscal situation in advance of this.

Meanwhile, the disdain and disinterest with which the British political system – led by rampant English nationalism – has treated Northern Ireland makes it clear there is little resistance from Britain to Irish reunification. There is a greater focus on the prospect of Scottish independence, which is also much more likely because of Brexit. Scottish people value membership of the European Union and voted heavily – as did Northern Ireland – to remain within the EU.

The drive for Scottish independence has been assisted by the perception that the Scottish National Party can be trusted to run its government. Devolution is perceived to have worked to the benefit of

Scotland. That surely is a message for Irish republicans – make Northern Ireland work better as a prelude to making a success of the call for Irish unity.

In our first edition, we made clear the extent of the failures of the Northern Ireland structures of governance. We pointed out the causes of the large subvention from the UK government: the cost of duplicated services because of social segregation; policy mistakes that have damaged economic performance; the weak education system; and the over-dependence on public sector employment.

Since our book was published, those arguments have been assisted by further collections of evidence. The new Pivotal think-tank published a report pointing out the massive scale of under-performance in the Northern Ireland public sector compared to that in Great Britain. Economic analysis by John FitzGerald and Edgar Morgenroth at Trinity College, Dublin, and by Seamus McGuinness and Adele Bergin of ESRI, have made clear the dead weight of economic failure in Northern Ireland.

In an interview about the first edition of the book on the BBC's Radio 4 Today programme I referred to Northern Ireland as a 'failed state'. This caused considerable negative reaction, so we might instead consider Northern Ireland to be a 'dysfunctional society'. The evidence for that in terms of mental ill-health, paramilitary crime, social dislocation and economic weakness is surely irrefutable.

Given that context, it should not be a surprise that increasing numbers of people from traditional unionist backgrounds now regard Irish unity as a preferable outcome – looking enviously at the way a theocracy in the south has become socially liberal, alongside a state that is economically successful.

It might be overstating it to say that Irish unity has become inevitable – but it does now look to be a question of when it will happen, rather than if. It seems clear that there is an implicit cross-party approach in the Republic to the question of unity: avoid support for unity referendums in the short-term, while preparing for them over the medium-term. There is now much greater levels of consideration about the process involved in a transition in the constitutional status of NI, alongside recognition of the type of investment required to make Northern Ireland into an economically and socially successful region.

It is surely no coincidence that the change in attitudes within Fine Gael and Fianna Fáil have come at the same time that a range of academic institutions are considering what the wording would be of referendums north and south, and who would be eligible to vote.

But there is another inescapable political reality. Only a broad political campaign can be successful. If it is perceived that Irish unity is a narrow 'Sinn Féin project' it cannot be successful. Genuinely non-partisan campaigning is required, drawing equally from all parts of the political spectrum – with convinced former unionists playing leading roles in explaining the benefits of economic, social and political integration across the whole island.

Increasing numbers of people born into traditional unionist communities are being persuaded of the opportunities presented by Irish unity. As the impact of Brexit becomes clearer – with Irish unity the route towards continued EU citizenship – then the support for a 'new Ireland' will grow.

The misleading claims made by the leave campaign in the Brexit referendum caused scepticism and hostility towards those who campaigned for leave, but also for the nature of a referendum campaign in which both sides were able to make grand claims without recourse to verifiable fact. It is essential that those mistakes are avoided when a referendum on Irish unity takes place.

We have reached a time to prepare for Irish unity. But it is not enough to achieve unity – we also have to make it a success. To do so it is essential to prepare. The intention of the second edition, as with the first edition, is to help with that process and to suggest steps to be taken for the preparations.

The ultimate objective – conceited though it might be – is to provide a plan that any political party or movement can take off the shelf and adopt. It is, quite simply, a programme for Irish unity.

Paul Gosling / February 2020

ACKNOWLEDGEMENTS

THE SECOND edition of 'A New Ireland' is the culmination of a project initiated and facilitated by Colm McKenna as research co-ordinator. It would not have happened without his dedication and determination. Huge thanks are given to Colm. Many others have helped with the project, but in particular Pat McArt for his ideas, contributions and sub-editing. Warm thanks are given to Richard Humphreys for permission to use his articles in the appendix and to Seamus McGuinness for his comments.

Note: all currency conversions reflected market values as at 9th February, 2020.

COVID-19 POSTSCRIPT

COVID-19 hit the world soon after this book was completed. It is a health emergency that is also an economic emergency and possibly a trigger for significant and permanent changes to the way our society is structured – how we socialise and how we work.

The crisis has also shown – as did Brexit – that the Irish government is better able to do strategic planning than are their London counterparts. Even committed loyalists respected the tone and compassion adopted by Leo Varadkar, as interim Taoiseach, in responding to the crisis and leading a path through it.

The coronavirus also illustrated the need to treat Ireland as a single geographic entity. Whatever happens with regard to the constitutional arrangements, it is clear that the response to this virus, as per foot and mouth in the past, needs to be managed on an all-island basis. In this, geographic isolation can be a strength, providing both jurisdictions have a single policy and practice in how they manage it.

As we emerge from the crisis, much of our economic life will be different from that in the past. We will surely continue to buy much more online, damaging physical retailing, reducing the size of our retail centres and increasing pressure for the online giants to increase the size of their tax payments to governments.

Around the globe, governments will need those tax revenues to invest in more effective health systems. In the case of Ireland, the arguments for cross-border health service integration to achieve efficiencies and enhance specialist service delivery are made even stronger.

Sectors that were a large part of our past economy will struggle to emerge from the crisis – parts of the retail sector, restaurants, pubs, hotels, airlines, airports, cruise liners and public transport will all have difficulty.

There will be opportunities and demands for increased provision of some goods and services. The online economy, with more people engaged with it at home, requires high quality broadband and a stronger electricity grid, supporting power-hungry data centres. Supply chains will be shortened, with 'near-sourcing' replacing globalised outsourcing of production. More Irish people will go on holiday in Ireland – visiting more places on the other side of the border from their homes.

Our economy is becoming digitised, including with payments increasingly made digitally. This is good for governments, which can use this to clamp down on the 'black economy' and improve tax revenue collection. It means that the closure programmes for bank branches will probably accelerate. Online security and data analytics will become even more important.

One serious risk is that social divisions will increase. Higher paid professionals working in the services sector in many cases can work as well and as productively from home as they can from an office. Not so poorer paid individuals, such as cleaners and taxi drivers. Those vulnerable workers typically have little or no savings and their situation has been made worse by the Covid-19 crisis.

What does all this mean for Irish unity? Socially, it seems likely that north and south will feel closer. The risk of contracting disease on a flight or a boat will for many people make Ireland feel a safer place to stay in, rather than travelling to Britain. That will strengthen social and economic links between the two jurisdictions.

Both Ireland and the UK – like the rest of the world - will have difficulties dealing with the cost of the coronavirus crisis. Whether this affects attitudes to Irish unity, it is difficult to predict. It seems likely that future British governments will seek to avoid unnecessary costs – increasing pressure from English politicians to reduce the subvention to Northern Ireland.

Similar arguments might be used in the Republic against integration of north and south. Alternatively, it could strengthen the arguments in this book for a period of transition – to use Van Morrison's phrase – in which Northern Ireland becomes a more modern, efficient and effective entity, modelling itself more on the advances made by the Republic in recent decades. And the economies of scale possible from successful unity could be seen as very attractive as we move forward.

Exactly what happens as a result of Covid-19 is, in truth, impossible to predict. Not least, at the time of writing, we do not know if a vaccination will be developed and whether immunity can be achieved. Without those facts, nothing is certain. For this author, however, the crisis does nothing to undermine his conviction that Irish unity is sensible, desirable and achievable.

Paul Gosling,
April 2020.

See also Appendix 1: Ireland Post Covid 19

STRENGTHS AND WEAKNESSES OF THE TWO JURISDICTIONS

NORTHERN IRELAND

STRENGTHS

- Higher education sector
- NHS (in principle)
- Good quality of life
- Low cost of living

WEAKNESSES

- Fragility of devolved government
- Weak Economy
- Brexit Impact
- Public sector dependency
- High level of economic inactivity
- Too few graduates/undergraduates
- Inadequate vocational skills
- Too many without basic skills
- NHS (in practice)
- Too little social housing
- Lack of effective sub-regional policy
- Low productivity
- Poor infrastructure
- Substantial fiscal deficit
- Declining manufacturing sector
- Small private sector services sector
- Low wages
- Absence of evidence-based policy

STRENGTHS AND WEAKNESSES OF THE TWO JURISDICTIONS

REPUBLIC OF IRELAND

STRENGTHS

- Stable government
- Strong economy
- Higher education sector
- Graduate skills
- High productivity
- Good infrastructure
- Falling fiscal deficit (near balanced budget)
- High, and growing, pay
- Open economy
- EU membership/EU funding
- High levels of FDI
- IFSC
- IDA
- Evidence-based policy making

WEAKNESSES

- High public debt
- Brexit impact
- Poor/expensive health service
- Too many without basic skills
- Too few homes
- Inadequate sub-regional policy
- High cost of living
- Vulnerability to global trading conditions/eurozone
- Threats to tax rate from EU & US

INTRODUCTION

THE CHALLENGES holding back the proper and full adoption of Strand One of the Good Friday Agreement have meant that we must now consider alternative options if it stalls yet again. Is the Stormont Assembly, as it is now constituted, sustainable and durable?

One option, clearly, is direct rule from Westminster, but that would only be tolerable to nationalists and republicans if, at the very least, there were a clear and specified consultative role for the Irish government. Returning to the old type of direct rule is unacceptable.

Another option, more acceptable to nationalists and republicans but not to unionists, would be a closer relationship between Stormont and the Dáil. Ultimately, this could lead to Stormont being either amalgamated with the Dáil, or else becoming a chamber within a federal structure in a new Ireland. These new arrangements would need to be under the auspices of the British Irish Intergovernmental Council.

If Stormont can survive, it needs to work better. This must involve a better working relationship with the Irish government. This could be assisted by regular cross border cabinet meetings.

But whatever happens in the near term, the economic and social weaknesses of Northern Ireland have to be fixed. It makes sense for the Republic to contribute to doing so, given the likelihood that at some point in the future there will be a united Ireland. Logically, this means that the Irish state should invest immediately in the road and rail infrastructure of Northern Ireland, in university expansion and vocational training.

This might be funded through the use of the Brexit contingency fund.

While the southern economy has outshone that of the north's, so too has its civic engagement. While the Civic Forum established under the Good Friday Agreement ground to a halt, the Citizens' Assembly in the Republic has been a massive success. This model needs to be replicated as a means of making greater and faster social progress in Northern Ireland. It can provide a way out of our cultural and social dislocation.

There are many aspects of cross-border society where progress is required. Given the nature of cross-border life and the reality of an open border, it is necessary to have much improved cross-border co-operation. It is absurd to pretend that matters like policing can be addressed on a silo basis separately by the Garda and by the PSNI. We need a genuine cross-border crime agency.

A NEW CONSTITUTION WOULD BE REQUIRED BASED ON AN AGREED BILL OF RIGHTS THROUGH THE CONSENSUS OF PERHAPS A CITIZENS' ASSEMBLY

The same approach is required for infrastructure planning, the development of our health service, enterprise development and food standards. Both jurisdictions are of a size where co-operation can improve service quality while reducing cost. This is no more than common sense. It does not in itself change the constitutional arrangements.

But the Good Friday Agreement was clear, that Irish unity will be achieved if and when that is the will of the majority of people in both the north and the south, as expressed in a referendum. That would require a new constitution, based on an agreed Bill of Rights. Sensibly its development would be based on conversations, involving unionists, seeking consensus perhaps through a Citizens' Assembly. Any such constitution will need to be flexible, changing as society evolves, but backed-up with the protections for the citizen from a Bill of Rights.

Whatever happens in terms of the constitutional settlement, it is also clear that the Northern Ireland subvention needs to be substantially reduced. That would be necessary for the Irish state to cover the cost burden of the north, if and when unity happens. But unionists must realise that the tolerance of UK taxpayers to the cost of Northern Ireland is moving to an end. If Northern Ireland is to remain within the United Kingdom, Whitehall will demand serious reform.

As we discuss the future, we need to focus on the objective – making life better for the majority of people across the island of Ireland. All proposals to address the hopes and fears of the people of the island need to be aspirational on an individual basis, future-orientated and realistic. Our belief is that the ideas espoused in this book are exactly that in ways

THERE ARE MANY ASPECTS OF CROSS-BORDER SOCIETY WHERE PROGRESS IS REQUIRED:

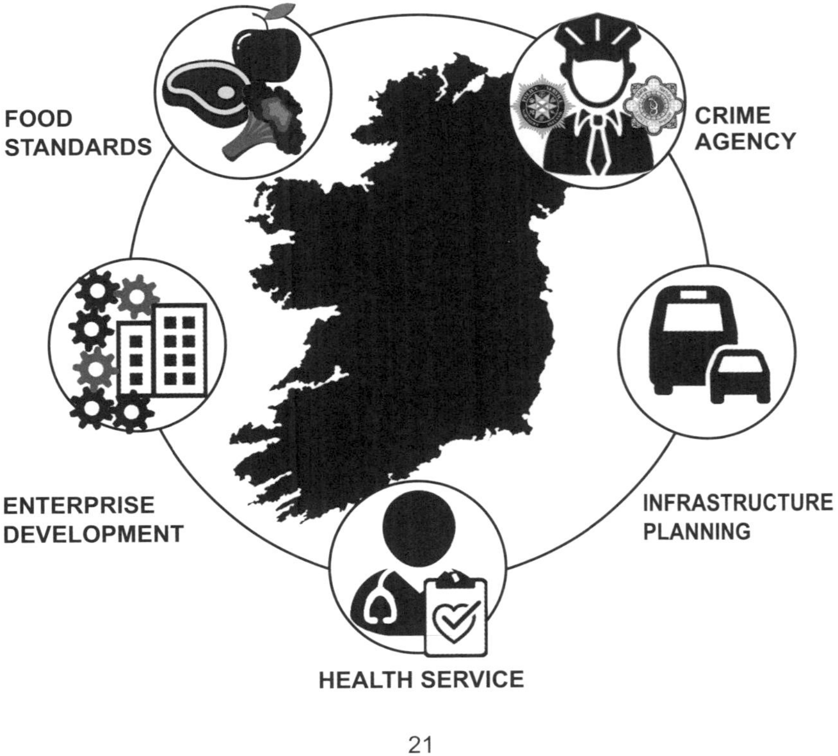

TOLERANCE OF UK TAXPAYERS TO THE COST OF NORTHERN IRELAND IS MOVING TO AN END

that can unite people through common goals.

Change is coming. What is at present unclear, is the nature of that change. But preparations for change are needed urgently.

Colm McKenna,
Research co-ordinator

1

THE TEN YEAR, TEN POINT PLAN

1 **NEGOTIATIONS SHOULD** begin to agree objectively the actual size of the UK's subvention to Northern Ireland in advance of any poll to initiate a united Ireland. The UK government would be asked to agree to continue its subvention to Northern Ireland for a temporary period, phasing this out on an annually tapering basis, with the UK subvention removed entirely within a negotiated period beyond reunification. UK support might be needed for up to ten years. Over the long term this would produce a significant fiscal saving for the UK, which is likely to be welcomed by taxpayers in GB. For Northern Ireland, the subsidy would be replaced by improved tax revenues as Northern Ireland benefits from the economic impact of reunification and the Republic's economic policies. Consideration could be given as to whether sovereignty might also transfer on a gradual basis. Stormont might continue to operate as a devolved assembly, but of Ireland rather than of the UK. There could be a phased move towards a truly all-island economy, with both sterling and the euro accepted by businesses during the transition process. Clarification is needed over responsibility for pension liabilities, both for former state and other public sector occupational pensions and for state pensions. Universities should begin research to consider how costs currently allocated by the Treasury to Northern Ireland should be divided post-Irish unity. Substantial efforts must be made to accommodate the fears and concerns of those who have a British or Ulster

British identity throughout the island of Ireland in order that a successful unified economy is achieved.

2 **INCREASED SPENDING** on capital projects in Northern Ireland is required to bring infrastructure up to modern European standards. The infrastructure deficit that was carried forward from the period of direct rule needs to be addressed, which means that the UK government has a moral obligation to help meet the cost of correcting the infrastructure deficit. A UK government investment of £10bn (€11.8bn) would assist significantly with this, towards the cost of roads, health reform, education facilities and water and sewage systems. This would recognise the absence of a 'peace dividend' following the Good Friday Agreement, which had been expected.

3 **A REDUCTION** in the number of public sector workers in Northern Ireland to the same proportion as the Republic and England would assist in making Northern Ireland financially self-sufficient. This would take place on a gradual basis to reduce the impact on individuals and on the wider economy. Ideally the impact would be spread over several years, achieved as much as possible by natural wastage. All redundancy, pension and restructuring costs would be met by UK. This restructuring would assist in boosting Northern Ireland productivity. This transition would be part of the phased withdrawal of UK support for Northern Ireland.

4 **IMPROVED DIRECT** links between education and industry in Northern Ireland as is the case in the Republic would lead to a more competitive market-oriented economy and increase employment rates.

5 **IDA IRELAND** would promote all of the island on the world stage. This would produce benefits for all. Given its track record in attracting FDI worldwide it should prove to be a major player in turning the Northern Ireland economy into a world class competitor. Invest Northern Ireland would be subsumed into IDA Ireland, with the merged body having a clear remit to promote sub-regional investment and economic development.

6 **NORTHERN IRELAND** needs to learn from the Republic with regards to elements of its education and skills system, which needs major reform in the north. The Republic needs to adopt an NHS-style, free at point of delivery, health system. Neither system is adequate at present. The Bengoa reforms[1] need to be implemented in Northern Ireland to eradicate long waiting times and waiting lists for diagnosis and treatment. An integrated all island health system, free at the point of delivery, is an essential prerequisite to achieving political integration. The Republic needs to accelerate its implementation of SláinteCare, the basis for a proper public health system.

7 **A HARMONISED** corporation tax rate is a necessary part of creating an all-island economy and would make all the island more attractive to foreign direct investment. This would also expand supply chains within, and across, the island, strengthening the internal economy in both the north and the south.

8 **A SINGLE** and integrated Ireland would create economies of scale and a more competitive economy. A single Ireland would be a world leader in the fields of research and development, higher education, pharmaceuticals and new technologies.

9 **A POLITICAL** agreement on a new all island jurisdiction, inside the EU, would attract renewed EU funding through Interreg, including financial assistance in restructuring Northern Ireland's infrastructure to improve its competitive position and integrated all-island economy.

10 **THE EUROPEAN UNION** would be asked to assist the reunification of Ireland, with Northern Ireland rejoining the EU. A special case should be presented to the European Union, and also to the United States, for assistance with the cost and social pressures involved with Irish reunification. This might be structured in ways that learn from the Marshall Plan and the experience of German reunification. A new 32 county administration should use low cost loans from the European Investment Bank to invest in the economy and all-island infrastructure.

2

THE ECONOMIC IMPACT OF BREXIT ON THE UK

EVEN BEFORE happening, Brexit had damaged the economy of the UK and of Northern Ireland. Uncertainty has blighted investment and optimism, as has the expectation that the UK will move away from alignment with EU regulations.

Impact of Brexit on the UK and Northern Ireland Economy by the end of 2020

Analysis by Bloomberg Economics concludes that the hit to the UK economy from Brexit is already greater than the UK's payments into the EU budgets over its entire 47 years of membership. The cost by the date of leaving had reached £130bn (€153bn), with a further £70bn (€82bn) impact likely by the end of 2020. It says the UK economy is currently (early in 2020) 3% smaller than it would have been without Brexit.[2]

There is a consensus amongst respected economists that Brexit is bad for the British economy – at least in the short to medium term. Professor Ray Barrell of Brunel University took the mainstream position of economists, saying "We now know the economy [of GB] will be between 2% and 6% smaller in ten years than it otherwise would have been."[3]

That is different from predicting that the British economy will contract, or enter recession, merely that it will not benefit from the growth that it otherwise would be expected to generate. If, however, the eurozone were to contract in that time, it is possible (if unlikely) that GB will avoid economic difficulties that it might have suffered from if it continued to be a member of the EU. Equally, it is possible that the whole of the EU will lose economic growth as a result of the Brexit decision.

According to UK government analysis, the Withdrawal Agreement with the EU will cut economic growth in the UK by 4.9% to 6.7% over a 15 year period, compared to projected growth remaining within the EU.[4]

It is worth considering the objectives behind Brexit. One of the most considered prospectuses for Brexit was put forward by the group styled as 'Economists for Brexit', which now call themselves 'Economists for Free Trade'[5]. Their most prominent members are Professor Patrick Minford of Cardiff University and Roger Bootle, head of Capital Economics. Both were influential advisors to Margaret Thatcher as prime minister, including over the ill-fated 'poll tax'.

Minford and Bootle are in the minority of economists who believe Brexit will be economically beneficial for the UK. Professor Minford has projected annual economic growth of 6.8% resulting from Brexit. Their proposals include replacing European markets with Asian markets; the adoption of unilateral free trade; moving away from basic manufacturing and focusing on services and high value manufacturing; lower regulation; lower taxes; lower minimum pay; and more investment in skills and infrastructure.

Minford and Bootle also propose a radical reshaping of the food and agriculture sector, ending food subsidies, buying more food on world markets, encouraging more farm land to be used for home building and so reducing housing costs. Their policies are of particular significance for Northern Ireland, given NI's much greater reliance on agriculture and food production and also on low value manufacturing. Northern Ireland has a much smaller services sector than GB.

The report from Ireland's Economic and Social Research Institute, authored by Seamus McGuinness and Adele Bergin *The Political Economy of a Northern Ireland Border Poll*, explains that while services provided 52% of the Republic's exports, in Northern Ireland the figure was just 18%.

In 2017, more than 70% of Northern Ireland's exports were in manufactured goods. In the same year, over 70% of UK GDP came from the services sector. UK government statistics for exports present a similar picture – total UK exports in 2017 were £634bn, of which £460bn (72%) were of services.

Manufacturing productivity in Northern Ireland is 38% higher than that across the Northern Ireland economy as a whole, according to a report conducted three years ago by Oxford Economics for Manufacturing NI. In the advanced manufacturing sector, productivity is 27% greater than in other parts of manufacturing production. This means that in advanced manufacturing, Northern Ireland matches GB levels, unlike in other parts of the economy where it lags. However, the UK as a whole is around 25% below the international average for manufacturing productivity.

It also worth remembering that the agri-food sector – including parts which are subject to cross-border production - accounts for £1bn out of the £3bn exports to the Republic and £1.3bn out of £6bn in sales to the EU as a whole."[6]

3
THE ECONOMIC IMPACT OF BREXIT ON NORTHERN IRELAND

WHILE THERE remains some uncertainty about the final shape of Brexit, it seems clear there will be a regulatory border in the Irish Sea. This will create limited trade barriers between Northern Ireland and Great Britain, including some bureaucratic obligations. Northern Ireland will effectively operate within the EU's Customs Union and Single Market. This will strengthen NI's economic relationship with the Republic of Ireland and the eurozone, while weakening it with Great Britain.

Brexit has already negatively impacted Northern Ireland's economy, in particular by damaging investment that would have flowed. According to Ulster Bank's chief economist for Northern Ireland Richard Ramsey, Northern Ireland entered recession in 2019.[7] The Northern Ireland Composite Economic Index[8] reported that the size of the region's economy in the third quarter of 2019 decreased by 0.1%. Over the prior year, output expanded marginally by 0.3%, a much smaller rate than UK growth of 1.1% - itself much lower than would likely have been the case without Brexit.

Northern Ireland's Exports: 2014

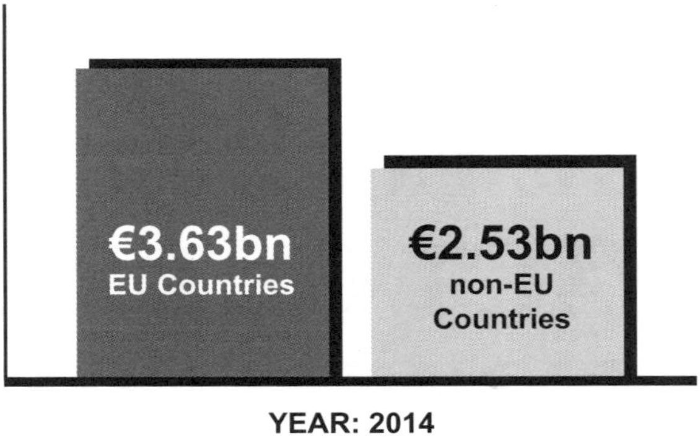

According to the European Parliament: "Northern Ireland is the part of the UK most distinctly affected by Brexit."[9] It pointed out: "Growth in exports to EU countries from Northern Ireland has considerably outpaced that to non-EU countries in recent years and amounted to £3.63bn in 2014, compared to £2.53bn of non-EU exports.... The importance of Northern Ireland's current tariff-free and quota-free trade relationship with the Irish Republic is apparent, with 34% of Northern Ireland's EU exports heading there (21% of the region's total exports). This makes Ireland the largest market for Northern Irish exports. More broadly, the majority of Northern Ireland's exports (57%) head to the EU."

GVA (gross value added) is regarded by many economists as a more relevant measure than GDP (gross domestic product).[10] Northern Ireland's GVA per person in 2018 was £22,428, which represented a fall of 0.5% from 2017 and is 78.7% of the UK average figure. This is the third weakest regional performance in the UK (behind Wales and North East England). In contrast, the UK GVA per person rose by 2.4% in 2017/18, suggesting that Northern Ireland suffered disproportionately from Brexit uncertainty, as well as political instability. The Ards / North Down area had the lowest GVA per person of any local area in the UK in 2018[11], a fact apparently influenced by commuting patterns[12].

The economic impact of the proposed Canada-style deal on the UK as a whole could be a loss of 5% of growth over the next 15 years, according to a leaked copy of the government's own analysis.[13] Given the lack of clarity over how Northern Ireland arrangements will work post-Brexit, it is impossible at present to suggest a credible prediction of how Brexit will impact the north's economy over future years. But there had been fears that a 'hard Brexit' could hit the north's potential output by 8%, reducing potential economic output by £3bn (£1,600 per person). If there were a pro rata reduction in employment, this could reduce potential employment by as many as 67,000 jobs.[14]

THE AGRI-FOOD SECTOR

The agri-food sector is particularly important for the Northern Ireland economy – and is especially at risk from Brexit. There are more than 29,000 farmers in Northern Ireland, who receive much more in EU Common Agricultural Policy (CAP) direct payments than from market prices.[15] Replacing CAP with a less generous system of farmer support payments could be a serious hit to Northern Ireland's economy. The European Parliament report suggests this could negatively affect Northern Ireland by £1.1bn a year.

"When measured across all farm types, average direct payments represented 80% of the value of average farm business income, 51% of the value of average cash income and 95% of the value of average net farm income for farms in Northern Ireland." says the Department for Agriculture, Environment and Rural Affairs, quoted by the UFU.[16] Total income from farming in 2019 was £290m, down from £386m a year before.[17] Northern Ireland's farmers receive one of the highest payments-per-hectare annual awards in the EU and 9% of the UK's total allocation of EU pillar payments.[18]

Brexit represents a threat on three levels to the farming sector. Firstly, there is the potential loss of labour, with many food producers at present reliant on workers from elsewhere in the EU because of the shortage of local labour willing to do this work. Secondly, there has been a significant increase in cross-border commercial operations in recent years, as agricultural and food producing organisations achieve economies of scale through cross-border mergers, such as Lakeland and Fane Valley. Food processing, in part as a result of this, can involve crossing the border repeatedly. Thirdly, there are fears that the eventual replacement of the Common Agricultural Policy is likely to lead to a loss of support to farmers generally[19] and to Northern Ireland farms in particular[20]. Brexit is a potential disaster for Northern Ireland's farmers and food producers, who are dependent on EU financial support.

Northern Ireland has received funding from a number of EU funding schemes[21]. These comprise the European Regional Development Fund, the European Social fund, the Regional Development Fund, Interreg, the Common Agricultural Policy, the Common Fisheries Policy and the Peace programme (currently Peace IV, which becomes Peace Plus). Once Northern Ireland leaves the EU it will be unable to receive several of these, though Peace funding is continuing. Should Northern Ireland become part of a united Ireland, it will again be eligible to receive EU funds.

In total, Northern Ireland will receive €3.5bn in EU funding between 2014 and 2020. Farming support currently funded by the EU will be replaced in England with new arrangements more focused on environmental protection.[22] It is likely that Northern Ireland will receive a smaller share of CAP funding in future which is relative to its population share of the UK, 3%, rather than its current 9% of the UK allocation of CAP. If that were to happen, it would be an annual loss of around half a billion euro coming into NI.

Farmers in Northern Ireland are particularly dependent on EU subsidies. The Northern Ireland Assembly explained: "the [EU's] Basic Payment Scheme currently accounts for 103% of the average Farm Business Income in Northern Ireland. The ending of such support could threaten the viability of many farms, particularly if there was neither a replacement or gradual wind down to enable readjustment.

"The income shock of removal of direct support could see a significant drop in the number of farmers. This could well create a rural unemployment impact that would extend beyond the farm gate as many rural shops and businesses indirectly benefit from farmers spending their BPS. There could also be a large scale abandonment of land if farmers go out of business and dereliction could also be a problem due to a lack of incentives to maintain environmental standards. A drop in the number of farmers could theoretically benefit those who managed to continue to operate as prices might rise for certain produce providing demand exceeded supply and farms might be able to expand if land became cheaper/available. This could make remaining businesses more profitable/efficient and potentially lead to employment generation."[23]

However, as the Assembly report adds, there is no certainty that the EU itself will continue with the CAP scheme, not least because of its cost. Policy on continued direct payments in the UK will be devolved to the national administrations, but it is unlikely this will be fully funded.[24]

It is worth noting that it is predicted that the UK's farming sector will shrink by perhaps around 15% as a result of Brexit. One academic, Dr. Michael Wallace of Newcastle University, projected that "close to 100%" of UK farms are likely to be worse off.[25]

Economists for Free Trade argue that abolition of CAP is one of the most important objectives of Brexit. "The CAP system leads to high food prices for UK consumers, increases inflation and reduces disposable income, which otherwise would boost consumer spending and thus the economy. Moreover, it artificially inflates agricultural land values, which further increases the cost of food and has wide knock-on effects to prices across the entire economy."[26]

Under policies influenced by Economists for Free Trade, there would be significant reductions in support payments for produce, as well as lower land values. This would be a double whammy for Northern Ireland farmers, though potentially freeing cheaper land for housing development. It is likely that agri-food exports from Northern Ireland to GB will anyway decline as a result of Brexit, with perhaps more food imported from around the world to take advantage of weaker regulation and greater economies of scale achieved in countries such as the United States, Argentina and Brazil.

UK government reform to CAP will reduce support payments to farmers, disproportionately affecting Northern Ireland. "Leaving the European Union and the CAP will give us the opportunity for fundamental reform," says a government consultation paper on farming support payments in England. "We want a more dynamic, more self-reliant agriculture industry as we continue to compete internationally, supplying products of the highest standards to the domestic market and increasing exports."[27] It adds: "We believe this is a vision that could work for the whole of the UK but we recognise that devolution provides each administration with the powers to decide its own priorities." But not, presumably, with devolved funding at current levels after 2020. "We therefore propose to further reduce and phase out Direct Payments in England completely by the end of the 'agricultural transition' period, which will last a number of years beyond the implementation period."

It is also worth noting the sub-regional impact of CAP payments within Northern Ireland. "£266.3m was paid out in single farm payments and £83.1m in rural development funding. ... Beneficiaries based in the Enniskillen area received the largest amount of CAP funding - £38.9m in total. This was followed by the Omagh area (£33.3m) and then the Ballymena area (£27.3m). The top ten town/city areas each received over £10m in EU payments – Enniskillen, Omagh, Ballymena, Newry, Dungannon, Armagh, Derry/Londonderry, Craigavon, Coleraine and Magherafelt. The majority of these towns/cities are west of Northern Ireland which is an area that historically struggles to attract as much funding as the east."[28]

4
A TALE OF TWO ECONOMIES

DAVID McWILLIAMS gained respect as the best known Irish economist to predict the global economic crash of 2007/8: he warned Irish property prices had become a bubble. He might now be the economist who reads it correctly about the financial benefit of Irish reunification. McWilliams examined the issue in some detail after Ireland's foreign affairs minister Simon Coveney said he would like to see a united Ireland in his lifetime.

McWilliams presented key economic statistics illustrating that since partition, the economies of the Republic and Northern Ireland have increasingly diverged.[29] The northern economy that was strong in 1922, is now weak. The southern economy that was weak in 1922, is now strong. "The union with Britain has been an economic calamity for Northern Ireland," said McWilliams. "All the people have suffered, Catholic and Protestant, unionist and nationalist."

He continued: "In 1920, 80% of the industrial output of the entire island came from the three counties around Belfast. Belfast was the biggest city in Ireland in 1911, larger than Dublin, and was home to Ireland's innovation and technology. At partition the North was industrial and rich, the South agricultural and poor....

"The Republic's economy is [now] four times larger, generated by a work force that is only two and a half times bigger. The Republic's industrial output is today 10 times that of the North. Exports from the Republic are 17 times greater than those from Northern Ireland, and

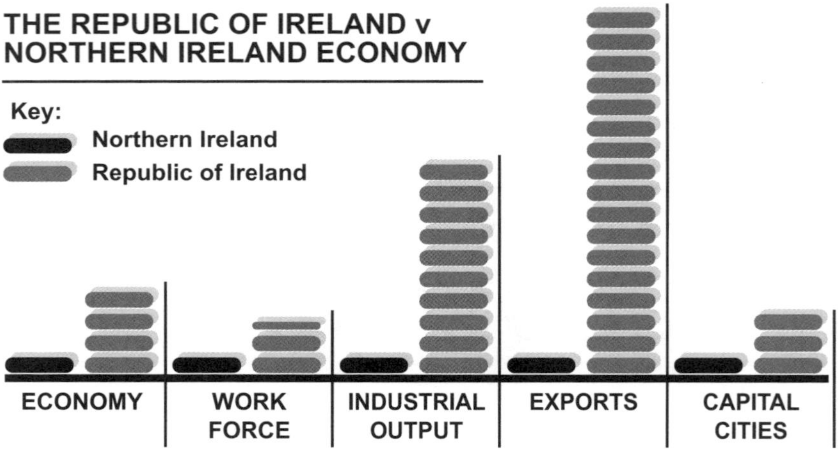

average income per head in the Republic, at €39,873, dwarfs the €23,700 across the Border.... Dublin is three times bigger than Belfast, far more cosmopolitan and home to hundreds of international companies."

McWilliams also pointed out – in an article published in the Belfast Telegraph - that while a peace dividend had been expected for Northern Ireland, it was actually delivered for the Republic. "Since the Good Friday Agreement, American corporations alone have invested close to $400bn in the Republic," he explained."[30]

Economies are often compared on the basis of GDP per person. In the case of the Republic, GDP per head is a flawed measure owing to the movement of capital and the transfer of asset ownership by multinationals domiciled in Ireland for tax reasons.[31] Ireland's Central Statistics Office is experimenting with the GNI (Gross National Income) measurement in place of GDP. EY's Neil Gibson observed that using this measure also demonstrated strong economic performance in the Republic. "Expressed per head, GNI is more than 10% higher [in RoI] than GDP per head in the UK and roughly 45% higher than GDP per head in NI."[32]

In Q3 of 2019, GVA per head in Ireland in 2015 was €52,461[33] (£44,542). By comparison in Northern Ireland it was £18,682[34], the third lowest of any UK region.[35]

Average full time income per head in the Republic in 2016 was £40,403

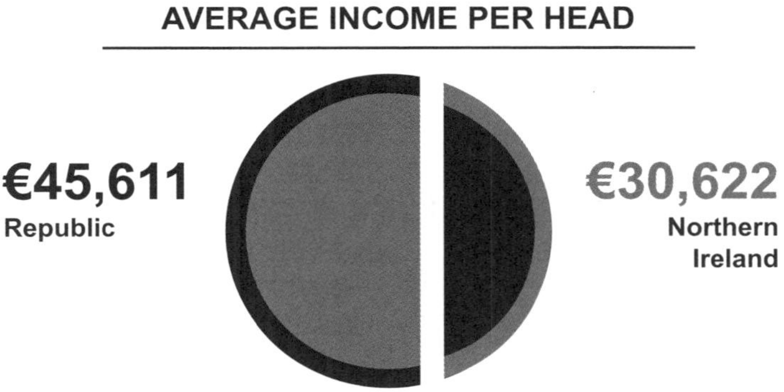

(€45,611[36]), compared to £25,999[37] (€30,622) in Northern Ireland. In other words, a worker in the Republic is typically paid half as much again as someone working in Northern Ireland.

Average pay is also higher in the Republic than in the UK as a whole.[38] Average weekly pay in the Republic in 2019 was €780.78[39] (£663). The average weekly pay in Northern Ireland in 2019 was £498[40] (€587). (Both statistics quoted are mean averages.) Public sector pay was higher than private sector pay in both jurisdictions: factors include qualification requirements; gender composition (women have pay equality in the public sector, but may face greater discrimination in the private sector) and trade union representation.

Disposable income is comparable in real terms north and south. In 2015, average household income by purchasing power parity was €13,300, in the border, midlands and western region of Ireland and €15,500, in the southern and eastern region (containing Dublin and Cork). In Northern Ireland in 2015, the figure was €15,400 per household. Pay figures in the north are flattered by the proportionately larger public sector. Disposable income in the south is reduced by expenditure on private health insurance: the same may apply in the future in the north if the current crisis in the NHS cannot be resolved.

Data analyst Peter Donaghy has considered regional income disparities across the island of Ireland. His conclusion is that the large conurbations attract the highest incomes: Dublin comes out at the top, followed by

Cork and areas around Dublin. While Northern Ireland tends to be poorer than the south, the Belfast commuting territories have higher average incomes than does Belfast city centre, and are comparable to much of the Republic. The poorest area in the island is Donegal, followed by western areas of Northern Ireland and the border areas of the Republic.[41] This suggests that partition is damaging for the both the Republic and the north.

Northern Ireland is at the time of writing in a significantly better position than the Republic in terms of unemployment. At the turn of the 2019/2020 year, unemployment in Northern Ireland was at an unusually low 2.3%, with the employment rate at 72.6%. Its economic inactivity rate remained the highest in the UK at 25.7%[42]. By comparison, in the Republic unemployment was 4.8%[43] and the employment rate was 69.6%[44]. The Republic is concerned that its employment participation rate is low by international standards and is developing policies to address this.[45]

The strength of the Irish labour market is, though, reflected in strong inward migration figures, with nearly 20,000 more people at work in the Republic now than before the global financial crisis.[46] [47] "Employment in Northern Ireland is forecast to contract slightly in late 2019 and early 2020, as slow growth and high-profile job losses filter through," predicted EY in the latter half of 2019.[48]

The recent very low unemployment statistics in Northern Ireland are peculiar, given the continuing weak state of its economy. One possible explanation is that low investment (exacerbated by Brexit) and consequent low productivity combined with low pay has generated higher demand for workers to compensate.

However, EY is positive about the recent employment record across the island. It said: "Employment is at a record high and ROI growth for 2018 comfortably topped the European growth charts. Despite there being no government in Northern Ireland [at the time of its report, 2019] , and the distraction that Brexit brings, firms across the island have enjoyed a remarkable growth story. There are over half a million more jobs across the island than there were six years ago. Outside of public administration and agriculture, all sectors have increased their employment and every county has seen job growth. With real incomes

now growing in both jurisdictions, the domestic economy is providing a significant boost to growth. Job growth is a leading economic indicator that politicians and the public recognise, and current levels are in stark contrast to a downbeat backdrop."[49] EY had predicted that had there been a no deal outcome from Brexit, the impact could have been 60,300 less jobs by 2022 across the island.

The Republic performs well in terms of quality of life.[50] However, there is an interesting divergence in analysis regarding equality and income disparity. The OECD concludes "there is a considerable gap between the richest and poorest – the top 20% of the population earn almost five times as much as the bottom 20%."[51] Yet, official statistics suggest a flatter income spread, with 62.6% of Irish households earning a gross income in 2016 of less than €60,000 a year, with 14.1% earning an income above €100,000.[52] Ireland has the lowest rate of tax of any EU nation for the lowest paid income earners.[53]

The Republic's economy is much more globally focused than is Northern Ireland's. Based on statistics from the International Monetary Fund's World Economic Outlook Database, Ireland's total Gross Domestic Product amounted to $324.3bn as of November 2016. Exports accounted for 39.5% of total Irish economic output.[54] For Northern Ireland, exports accounted for 20% of output (as measured by GVA), which is above the UK level of 17%. The Republic of Ireland is NI's largest export destination (31% by value), with the EU as a whole (excluding GB) responsible for 55% (by value) of NI's exports.[55] The Republic's global focus makes it much more vulnerable than the UK to global shocks, but much better positioned to take advantage of global growth.

Irish economic policy in the 1990s was the basis for remarkable growth. "EU membership, and the single market programme of the late 1980s and early 1990s, were essential in allowing Ireland to finally reap the full economic rewards of its independence," wrote Kevin O'Rourke

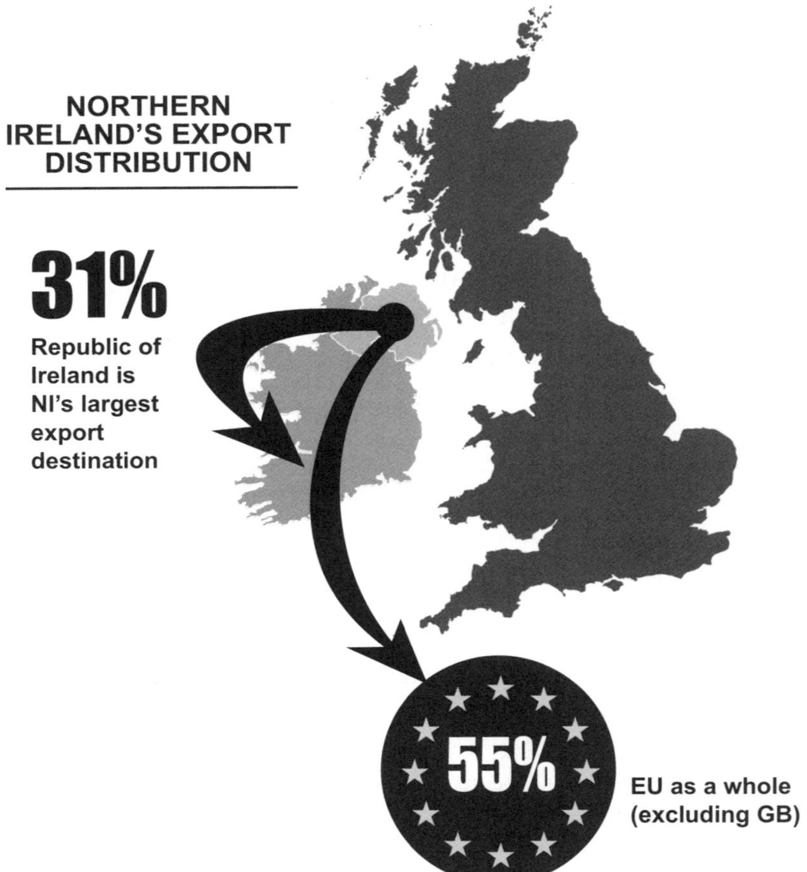

in a 2016 Oxford University paper. "The policy mix that we adopted is well known: a low corporation tax and other incentives for inward investment, including investment in education and infrastructure."[56] The author adds that social partnership, wage restraint, stable industrial relations, political independence and EU membership were all part of an attractive policy environment.

"Underpinning everything was two crucial factors: our political independence, which allowed us to adopt a policy mix well suited to our own circumstances; and our membership of the European single market, without which none of this would have worked."[57] While economic policy was subject to some major errors (such as weak banking regulation), which exposed Ireland disproportionately to the global crash of 2008, it is clear that Ireland had a fundamentally strong economy – strong enough, in fact, to deal with the punishing regime of bailing-out its failed banking system.

WIDENING ECONOMIC GAP

In recent years, the economic gap between the south and the north has widened. EY's Economic Eye study for summer 2018[58] reported that while economic growth in the Republic in 2017 was 7.8%, in Northern Ireland it was a mere 1.6%. The Central Bank of Ireland remains positive about the economic outlook for the south despite Brexit. Its Quarterly bulletin for Q4 in 2019 said: "If a disorderly, no-deal Brexit can be avoided, it is projected that underlying economic activity will grow at a relatively solid pace in coming years.... In the event of a deal, GDP growth is forecast to be 5% in 2019, 4.3% in 2020 and 3.9% in 2021."[59]

According to EY, factors behind the strong Irish performance include being well positioned to benefit from global economic growth – which Northern Ireland may not be. Mike McKerr, EY Ireland's managing partner, commented: "The RoI economy is generating significant momentum suggesting some resilience to Brexit, though it differs across sectors and locations. The retail and consumer sector appears to face a profoundly challenging time in Northern Ireland." EY has been much optimistic about the prospects for the Republic than for Northern Ireland. "The headline data suggests an increasing divergence in economic fortunes across the island. The Republic of Ireland sits atop the European growth charts, while Northern Ireland is closer to the bottom."[60]

HOW THE DIFFERENCE IS EXPLAINED

There are a variety of reasons for the difference in economic performance since partition. Clearly, the Troubles was one factor. This damaged the economy of Northern Ireland and of border counties in the Republic, particularly Donegal. The Good Friday Agreement failed to deliver the 'peace dividend' at the levels expected.

Partition has been damaging to the whole of Ireland, especially the border region. The economic damage to border areas has eased, but remains noticeable. Average disposable incomes in Donegal and the north east border areas rose from 75.6% of the Irish national average in 1973 to 92.5% in 1994, and in 2002 it was around 90%.[61] Statistics published by the EU on average regional pay shows the Republic's border, midland and western region still has average pay below that of the southern region.[62] It is to be hoped that reunification would increase the focus of the new state on Donegal and other border areas – not least because road transport connections from Dublin to Donegal would no longer need to cross an international boundary.

The continuing situation is well described by the Irish Borderlands website, published by Queen Mary College, part of the University of London[63]. "The borderlands of Northern Ireland and Ireland are amongst the most disadvantaged and deprived areas of the island. Though places near the border's eastern region, including the cities of Newry in Northern Ireland and Dundalk in Ireland, have recently grown in prosperity as part of the Belfast-Dublin axis of development, most of the borderlands were badly affected by the Troubles and continue to suffer the significant negative economic and social effects of the border. As in other contexts, the creation of a border in an area previously traversed by long-standing and multiple networks – familial, social, economic – dramatically distorted or destroyed these existing links and interconnections. While some pre-partition social networks continued on a cross-border regional or all-island basis, for many people old patterns of family connections and friendships were broken, severely curtailed, or a struggle to maintain."

A more fundamental economic reason over the longer-term for the difference in performance relates to the different sectoral focus of the two economies. At partition, Northern Ireland was dependent on heavy engineering, such as shipbuilding, and on shirt making. These industries have been badly affected by globalisation and Northern Ireland has been only partially successful in stimulating replacement industrial sectors.

The UK economy has refocused away from manufacturing to the

service economy. This has tended to increase inequality and the wealth divide in the UK. London has prospered, while regions that have traditionally been more dependent on manufacturing have suffered.[64] The 'Great Recession' increased regional disparities, with London recovering more strongly and more quickly than have other, weaker, regions.[65]

The restrictive nature of devolution for Northern Ireland limited the regional assembly's capacity to develop its own industrial strategy that reflected its distinctive needs – recovering from the collapse of the shipbuilding and linen sectors – and the challenge of geographical marginalisation. "The inability of the new Northern administration to deviate in any significant way at all from UK-wide policy simply reflected the extremely limited scope for local autonomy that was provided for in the 1920 Government of Ireland Act under which its local parliament (Stormont) operated," argued John Bradley in his important analysis *The History of Economic Development in Ireland, North and South*.[66]

Northern Ireland's economic decline resulted from the lack of international investment because of the Troubles and the "serious crisis" in economic policy in the north.[67] Northern Ireland "tracked" the manufacturing decline of the UK as a whole, but without generating a new private services sector to compensate, asserted Bradley.

Northern Ireland instead became increasingly reliant on the public sector for employment, with a big growth in public sector employment between the mid 1960s to the late 1980s.[68] With Northern Ireland having a higher corporation tax rate than the south, the north's inward investment has tended towards low cost support services, rather than profit centres. Multinationals have tended to prefer to locate profit centres in the Republic, where they can pay a significantly lower rate of corporation tax. (It should be noted that the Republic's corporation tax advantage is being challenged both by proposals from the European Commission and US tax reforms, which make Irish tax residency less attractive for corporations. Despite this, the Republic is still very attractive from a corporate tax perspective.)

The Republic has benefited from IDA Ireland (formerly known as the Industrial Development Agency), which has been assisted by the low rate of corporation tax to be much more effective than the north's Invest

Northern Ireland in attracting foreign direct investment (FDI). But multinationals have been attracted to Ireland not just because of the tax rate: other factors include a highly skilled and motivated labour market; a welcoming culture for migrant workers and managers; the English language (an important advantage with regards to attracting US investment destined for the EU); and substantial investment in infrastructure (particularly in the big cities). It is important to note that another important factor has been IDA's ability to influence government policy, for example to improve roads infrastructure to assist with attracting FDI to regions away from Dublin.

The perception in Northern Ireland is that Invest Northern Ireland does not have the same policy influence, with the result that there are high levels of unemployment and lower levels of inward investment in the north west of NI. This policy was reinforced by the Barnett review of economic policy which endorsed "the importance of government policy not seeking to unduly influence the location of FDI within NI".[69]

"RoI in recent decades has performed well globally in attracting inflows of foreign direct investment (FDI), despite challenging economic circumstances," reported a Northern Ireland Assembly research paper.[70] It added that FDI was disproportionately attracted to Dublin and Cork, with less investment attracted to other cities and regions. However, following the global crash, IDA was given a target of 50% of new investment being located outside these two cities.

In 2019 IDA Ireland attracted foreign investments in 250 projects, generating 21,844 new jobs, with the result that 245,096 people in the Republic are employed by overseas businesses, with the support of IDA.[71] By comparison, Invest Northern Ireland 'promoted' 5,600 new jobs in the 2016/17 year,[72] rising to 9,033 new jobs in 2018/19[73]. The past clear and strong difference in performance between the two agencies may now be levelling off, but this needs to be assessed over a longer time period. Anyway, performance may be less to do with the competence of the two agencies and more to do with more effective policy levers being applied in the Republic.

The Republic has been clever in its targeting of growth sectors, particularly those that prosper in a globalised economy. RoI has an open economy, from which it is easy to trade internationally. As a committed

FOREIGN DIRECT INVESTMENT (FDI)

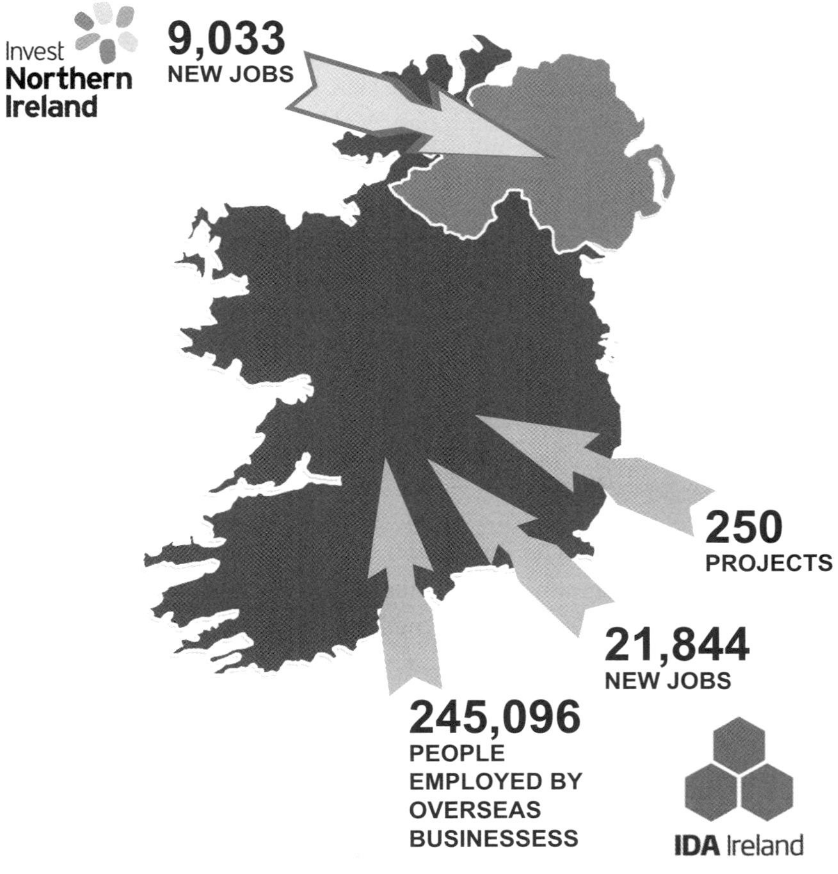

member of the European Union, the Republic has benefited from investment from both within and outside the EU. Ireland is recognised by investors from countries outside the EU – particular the United States, but also other countries such as Israel – as an excellent bridgehead into the EU. But the second largest foreign investment source is Germany[74], above the UK's level of investment and helps explain why 'Irexit' has little traction in Ireland. Dublin's International Financial Services Centre has been a major success, attracting banks, accountancy firms and fund managers, and acting as the major global base for various niche activities, such as aircraft leasing.

Current factors affecting RoI growth include: Brexit relocations from London; continuing foreign direct investment from the United States, despite US tax cuts; the effectiveness of IDA Ireland; the low corporation tax rate; the strong skills base; Ireland's ability to attract global talent, both Irish returners and others, because of strength of economy, the character of existing FDI, and increasingly socially liberal society; a focus on key sectors, including IT, pharmaceuticals and activities with profit centres; Ireland's integration into the global economy; and the attractiveness of Ireland to the financial services sector – the speaking of English, tax rates, an even lower effective tax rate, and the strong cluster of professional firms specialising in the financial services sector that are based in Dublin's International Financial Services Centre. Ireland's political stability, compared to the systemic instability in Northern Ireland, is another positive.

There are a number of variations in terms of public policy between the two jurisdictions. The Republic of Ireland's corporation tax rate is 12.5% (some corporations have been able to avoid even this). Northern Ireland is subject to the UK rate, which is currently 19%. While outline agreement between the main parties was achieved for Northern Ireland to match the Republic's rate, the failure of those parties to achieve a sustainable and continuing administration meant the lower rate was not implemented. The revived Stormont Executive has indicated this is not a priority.[75]

There is a greater focus on skills and qualifications in the Republic than in Northern Ireland. While 45% of young people in the Republic complete their education with a degree or higher, this is true of only about 31% in Northern Ireland.[76] More than a third of Northern Ireland school leavers who go on to university do so in Great Britain, most of whom do not return to work in Northern Ireland.[77] While 26% of Northern Ireland's adult working age population are graduates, the figure is over 35% in Dublin and Cork.[78] Both the Republic and Northern Ireland suffer from a problem of too many adults being without basic skills.

PRODUCTIVITY

According to PwC, the Republic of Ireland is around 60% more productive than is Northern Ireland.[79] Productivity across the UK has been a challenge in recent years, holding back recovery after the Great Recession. But productivity is a significantly greater challenge in Northern Ireland than in Great Britain. "Whilst productivity has slowed at national [UK] level and the UK has lost some ground relative to competitor nations, the gap between Northern Ireland and the UK average has been persistent and widening for many years despite being the target of a number of economic strategies," observed Ulster University.[80] It added: "GVA per head in Northern Ireland is only 75% of the GB average. This means that there is a 25% productivity gap between the GB and NI."[81]

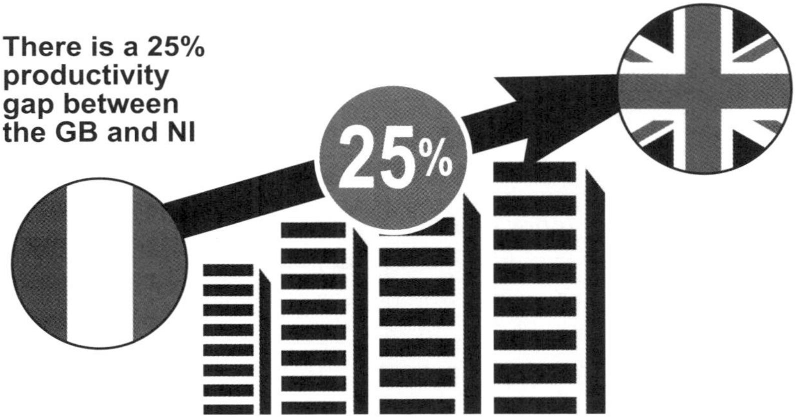

Moreover, there is a worrying variation in productivity levels within Northern Ireland, which points to policy neglect in terms of the sub-regions within the north. The UK has the fifth weakest productivity within the G7[82], with Northern Ireland some 17% below the UK average[83], but Belfast is 12% below UK average, the west and south of Northern Ireland 20% below the UK average and the north of Northern Ireland about 23% below the UK average.[84] (The north of Northern Ireland NUTS III area comprises the Derry City and Strabane District Council and Causeway Coast and Glens District Council areas.[85])

There are a number of factors that dictate the level of economic productivity, most of which come down to policy decisions, including investment. The UK's 'productivity handbook' named five factors as being critical in determining productivity growth. These are investment, innovation, skills, enterprise and competition.[86]

Private sector investment has lagged because Northern Ireland has been insufficiently attractive to international investment, while also not producing enough high margin indigenous businesses. In part, this is a circular argument – investment is not attracted to locations that have the reputation and reality of suffering from low productivity. Moreover, footloose capital is typically attracted to a low tax jurisdiction, other factors being equal.

The lack of public sector investment is arguably at least equally relevant in the case of Northern Ireland. It has significant infrastructure deficits, including roads, rail, water services and digital connectivity. This damages productivity as it takes longer to get goods to market, for executives to travel to meetings and for commuters to get to work. Without adequate sewage systems it is impossible to progress major new developments, including the Belfast City Deal. The lack of fast broadband speeds in rural areas of Northern Ireland is a major impediment.

The absence of innovation is itself the result of a combination of factors: the lack of foreign direct investment; the limited tax incentives to locate state-of-the-art private sector R&D facilities in Northern Ireland; the small size of the university sector (the number of Northern Ireland school leavers going on to university elsewhere would be sufficient to populate an additional university in Northern Ireland[87]); and the absence of a more competitive commercial environment.

Northern Ireland lacks skills at all levels: it has too few graduates; it has a shortage of technical vocational skills; and it has too many people without basic skills. The Nevin Economic Research Institute explains: "The skills deficit in Northern Ireland is sizeable and enduring and the most worrying statistic is for those with no level 1 National Vocational Qualifications. NVQ stratifies a range of qualifications ranging from GCSEs to trade apprenticeships and university degrees. In 2015, 16% of 16 to 64 year olds did not have a level 1 NVQ. To have less than a level 1 NVQ means less than 5 GCSEs at A-C grade."[88]

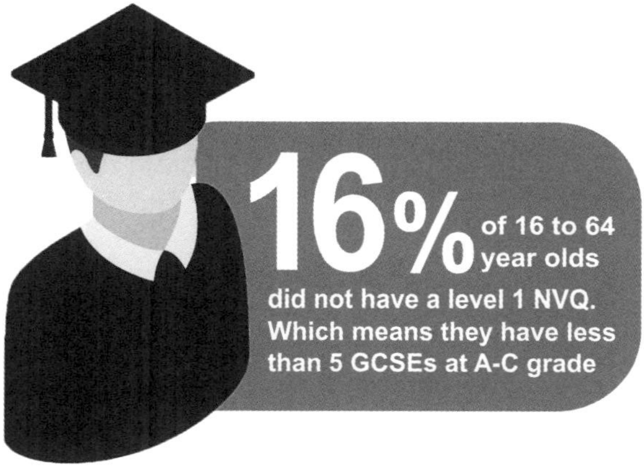

With a sub-par economy, people with the best skills tend to be attracted elsewhere, leaving behind those with inadequate skills – for whom other places are not welcoming. In effect, the market works in ways that leave the least skilled people in Northern Ireland, without offering sufficient incentives to retain or attract those with the highest skills. With private sector pay lagging behind that of the public sector, more than half of graduates in Northern Ireland are attracted to work in the public sector.[89]

The issue of enterprise is a regular bug-bear for Northern Ireland. Too few new businesses are created in Northern Ireland and too few of those that are set-up survive. Northern Ireland has the weakest entrepreneurial environment of the UK's four nations and the lowest rate of new business start-ups. "The distribution of TEA [Total early-stage Entrepreneurial Activity - the intention to start a business] rates in 2015 was similar across the home nations: England at 7.2%, Wales at 6.8%, Scotland at 6.7% and Northern Ireland at 5.4%".[90] "Northern Ireland is the one UK region where businesses births and deaths (registration and deregistration) were almost equal, at roughly 9% of registered businesses in 2014; the UK business birth rate in 2013 was 14.1% and the death rate was 9.7%. Since 2009, Northern Ireland has been persistently below the rest of the UK in terms of the net change in the number of business registrations, with an annual decline in the total number of businesses registered."[91]

One of the major challenges for the Northern Ireland economy is the lack of progression from small to large. If more small firms could become large, then Northern Ireland would have a bigger and more competitive economy. Instead, the indigenous economy is dominated by small firms. "Small and medium-sized companies and self-employed people, together, provide 75% of employment, 75% of turnover and 81% of GVA in NI's private sector. Furthermore, SMEs actually employ more people than NI's large companies and the public sector combined."[92]

It can be argued that these problems relate to a significant extent to the small size of Northern Ireland, with a population of just 1.8 million people and a land border to the south and a sea border to the east. There are cost barriers to competing with Great Britain and trade barriers – some regulations and differences in tax regimes – with the Republic of Ireland. Becoming a more integrated part of a larger all-island economy can be expected to generate a more competitive environment, strengthening productivity in the process.

CBI Northern Ireland director Angela McGowan was referenced in the Sunday Business Post as arguing that many companies in Northern Ireland have operated on all-island basis for over 20 years, allowing them to enjoy higher growth, greater efficiencies, a larger customer base and wider pool of suppliers.[93]

Policy-based causes of weak productivity would presumably be addressed by government and corrected post-reunification. This would lead to a gradual levelling-out of economic performance between the Republic and Northern Ireland.

John FitzGerald has examined the issue of weak Northern Ireland productivity in an article in the Irish Times. He explained: "The low investment rate in the North has been translated into a steady fall in labour productivity, measured as output per person employed, relative to the UK average. Between 2000 and 2014, the North's productivity fell from 93% of the UK average to 80%. What makes that even worse is that the UK's productivity has itself been declining over the last decade relative to European Union partners. So the North has been experiencing a falling share of a falling index."[94]

Politics (and economics) is often about making assumptions. The assumption of this author is that following an extended period of austerity in GB, a generous confidence and supply deal with the DUP and a one-off deal from the UK government involving a £1bn additional fiscal transfer to Northern Ireland for the New Decade New Approach agreement, that there will be a point where UK government generosity towards Northern Ireland recedes. At some time it is likely that Northern Ireland will suffer GB levels of reduced public spending. Moreover, Brexit will inevitably lead to a significant change in economic focus, which will have a major impact on NI. There needs to be a rise in Northern Ireland levels of productivity, which is likely to involve a further reduction in the public sector headcount. So the conversation should not be about comparing a united Ireland with the status quo – rather comparing two alternative future visions of where Northern Ireland society moves towards.

THE INFRASTRUCTURE DEFICIT

Northern Ireland's infrastructure is inadequate and is a key factor in its weak productivity. Evidence for this is clear: long commuting times in Belfast, limited motorway and rail connectivity, poor road connections in the North West and large parts of the rural areas without fast broadband speeds.

The House of Commons Northern Ireland Affairs Select Committee warned in 2017 that "Without urgent investment in Northern Ireland's energy infrastructure, the industry is not confident it will be able to keep the lights on after 2021."[95]

In summer 2016, a joint report from the CBI and Ibec argued for improved infrastructure to support the all-island economy. Its priority was a major upgrade to create a modern, all-island, road network that connected all key urban centres, including the link between Dublin and the north west of Ireland, Sprucefield by-pass to improve the connection between Dublin and Belfast and an upgrade between Sligo and Letterkenny. It argued that these improvements would "embed peace and prosperity" and help "to bring economic opportunities and prosperity to every region, locality and community."[96]

Northern Ireland's Investment Strategy plans for a capital spend on infrastructure projects of £8.2bn for the five year period 2015/16 to 2020/21. Priorities include £1.2bn for road projects (including the Belfast to Derry, and Derry to Dublin connections, Belfast's York Street

AN ALL-IRELAND INFRASTRUCTURE

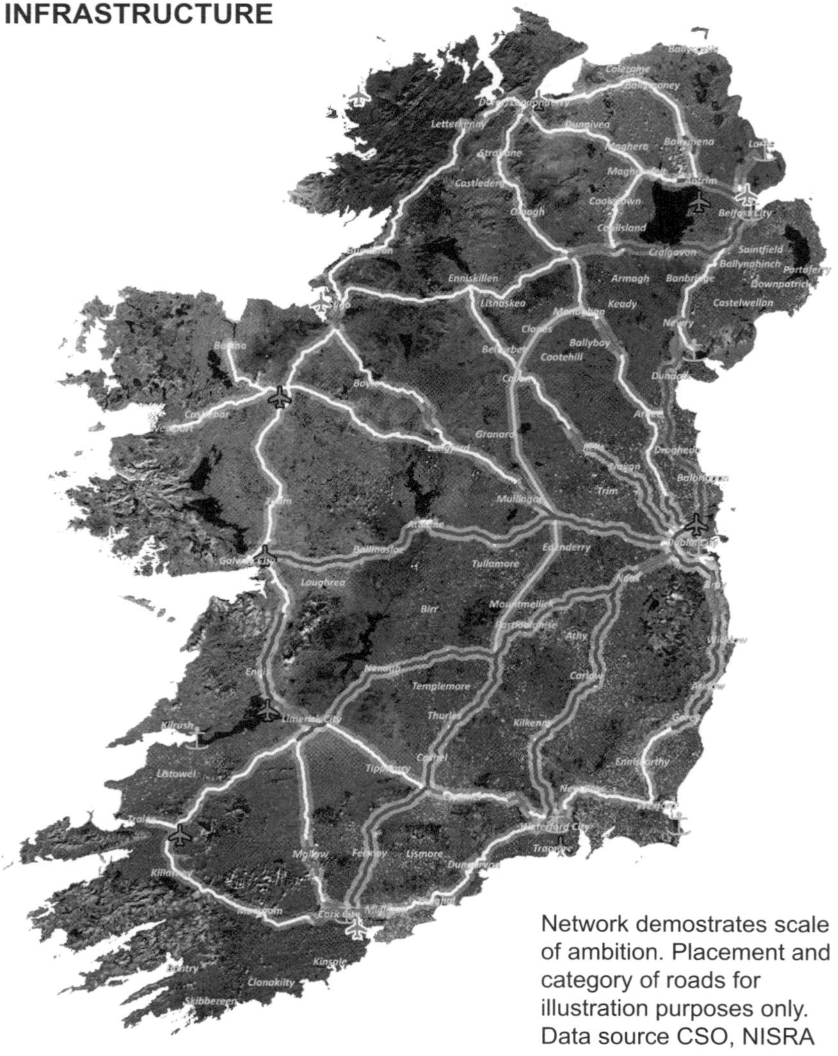

Network demostrates scale of ambition. Placement and category of roads for illustration purposes only. Data source CSO, NISRA

interchange and the Belfast to Larne road); £1.9bn for healthcare buildings (hospitals, primary care, etc); £1.2bn on schools; £1bn on water and waste water; and £855m on housing.[97] The Northern Ireland Audit Office has pointed out that a number of major infrastructure projects have hit serious difficulty, suggesting a lack of project management capability.[98]

This can be contrasted with the much more ambitious €116bn infrastructure investment plan[99] for the next decade published by the Irish government. This potentially provides one of the EU's highest levels of publicly funded infrastructure investment. While it is true that there are also contributions from motorists to road funding through tolls in the Republic, it may be that northern motorists and businesses might be willing to pay tolls if these lead to higher investment and shorter journey times.

However, planned investment is insufficient to address Northern Ireland's existing infrastructure deficit. Northern Ireland's weak infrastructure is, in part, the result of inadequate investment during direct rule years: it can therefore be argued that the UK government should contribute to addressing this deficit.

NORTHERN IRELAND'S TRADING RELATIONSHIP WITH GREAT BRITAIN

In 2016, 15% of Northern Irish sales and exports of goods and services beyond its own geographical borders went to the Republic of Ireland.[100] This had a value of around £4.3bn[101], representing 5% of total Northern Ireland production[102] and 35% of NI's exports outside the UK[103]. The value of trade to the north from RoI was worth much less to the Irish economy, at around £1.3bn.[104] Northern Ireland's exports of goods to the whole EU, including RoI, was about £7.8bn in 2016.[105] Northern Ireland's sales to GB were of much greater value, at about £15bn. This compares to internal sales within Northern Ireland, of about £50bn.

However, much of Northern Ireland's sales to GB contain materials or ingredients sourced from the Republic, via integrated supply chains: Brexit therefore threatens the basis of much of Northern Ireland trade with GB.[106] Moreover, one and a half times more Northern Ireland businesses sell to the Republic than sell to GB.[107] Exports are more important to Northern Ireland than to GB: they constitute 20% of Northern Ireland output, compared to 17% of the UK as a whole.[108] These factors demonstrate the need for Northern Ireland businesses to be able to trade freely with both GB and RoI, both post Brexit and post reunification. Reduced trade either west to east or north to south would be extremely negative for NI.

The big questions, then, are: what will happen to Northern Ireland sales to GB with border controls in the Irish Sea?; would Northern Ireland's sales to GB significantly fall if Northern Ireland left the UK and became part of a united Ireland?; would sales to RoI and the rest of the EU increase at a scale to compensate for that?; and would a gradual transfer from being part of the UK to being part of a United Ireland mitigate the negative impact on sales to GB? It is important that an economic plan be drawn up to consider how traders in Northern Ireland could either continue to trade at the same level with GB after reunification, or else replace that trade with the EU. It is important that Northern Ireland maintains a close relationship with GB, whether or not it becomes part of a united Ireland. That could best be achieved by avoiding tariffs, minimising border controls and to support trade to continue to be conducted in sterling, as well as euro.

According to analysis from the Northern Ireland Assembly[109] the top five exported commodity groups from Northern Ireland in 2017 were machinery and transport (£2.88bn, 33.7%); chemicals (£1.42bn, 16.7%); food and live animals (£1.34bn, 15.7%); other manufactured items (£1.31bn, 15.3%); and manufactured goods (£0.76bn, 8.9%). It is impossible to predict to what extent these goods exports to GB would continue following a united Ireland. There would be a particular challenge for Northern Ireland's manufacturing sector, which sells more goods into GB than it does into Northern Ireland, RoI and the rest of the EU combined.[110]

THE FITZGERALD ANALYSIS

John FitzGerald and Edgar Morgenroth's paper *The Northern Ireland Economy: Problems and Prospects* was published by Trinity College Dublin.[111] It provides a scathing analysis of the performance of the north's economy.

The central tenet of their argument is that the north's economic weakness flows from its skewed education system. "The failure to reform the education system to reduce the number of early school leavers and increase the numbers of graduates is the single most important factor in the low growth," the authors conclude.

The authors warn –as did the first edition of this book – that Northern Ireland should not assume that the level of subvention via the Barnett Formula will continue indefinitely. "Brexit will, undoubtedly, have serious negative consequences for the Northern Ireland economy. Possibly more serious for Northern Ireland are the changes taking place in the politics of the UK which could see a reduction in transfers in the future."

FitzGerald and Morgenroth conclude that: "The best economic outcome for Northern Ireland is one where future UK governments commit to providing continuing large transfers to Northern Ireland for at least a further decade in return for a change in regional economic policy aimed at promoting economic growth. Public expenditure needs to be reallocated from sustaining consumption, especially public services, to investing in education and infrastructure. While painful initially, it would move the Northern Ireland economy onto a sustainable growth path."

The paper argues that administrations in Northern Ireland – and UK direct rule ministers – are guilty of "frittering away" financial support from London on policy failures that did not address the province's underlying structural weaknesses.

Two core policy changes are required to strengthen Northern Ireland's economy, but the positive impact will take several years to be felt, says the paper. It argues: "The best economic option for Northern Ireland is that it is given many years to put its economy in order. If the transfer rate were sustained for a decade, and if... there was a major reallocation of public resources in Northern Ireland to promote a more productive economy, this could help move the Northern economy onto a sustainable growth path.

"Substantial savings will need to be realised in areas of public expenditure to free up resources for other necessary investment. The second level school system needs to be rationalised to replace the current system, where children are selected by ability at age 11, with a system that is inclusive of children of mixed ability, providing genuine equality of opportunity for children from disadvantaged backgrounds. In addition to investing to ensure higher completion rates in high school, significant investment in third level education is needed to expand the number of students studying at third level institutions in Northern Ireland. The fact that a quarter of young people attend university in GB and that two thirds of these end up as emigrants when they graduate, taking jobs outside Northern Ireland, highlights the importance of such an expansion. In addition, resources need to be reallocated to infrastructural investment to support increasing productivity and output across Northern Ireland.

"The failings identified in the report on the competitiveness of Northern Ireland need to be addressed. In addition, the factors that discourage emigrants from Northern Ireland returning, especially those emigrants with third level education, need to be identified and tackled. These obstacles to returning go beyond the realm of economics."

FitzGerald and Morgenroth conclude that Irish unification is unaffordable in short-term because of the scale of economic failure in Northern Ireland. This argument is considered in more detail in a later chapter.

THE ESRI ANALYSIS

A more positive analysis of the prospects for Irish unity was put forward by ESRI, the Economic and Social Research Institute for which FitzGerald was previously research professor. The recent ESRI paper *The Political Economy of a Northern Ireland Border Poll*[112] was written by Seamus McGuinness and Adele Bergin.

This paper, contrary to FitzGerald and Morgenroth, recognises that the key to Irish unity is to achieve it via an organised transition. The authors comment:

"Advocates of a border poll must outline strategies that can reduce the subvention requirement, through increased productivity, and provide an honest assessment of the time-period over which this can be achieved. In all likelihood, any re-unification will require a transition period during which both operational and fiscal responsibilities will be gradually transferred from the UK to the RoI. It is unclear how long any transition

The ESRI Analysis uses the transfer of sovereignty of Hong Kong from the UK to China.

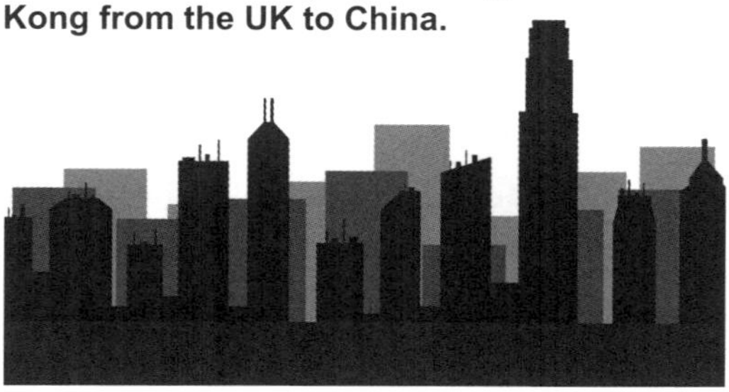

period should last as there are few insights available from a historical perspective. One potential indicator is the transfer of sovereignty of Hong Kong from the UK to China, which occurred in 1997, some 13 years following the signing of the Sino-British Joint Declaration in 1984. Arguably, a negotiated transition period would allow both the UK and Irish governments' an opportunity to co-ordinate policy to allow for a gradual re-integration which should also involve the introduction of new education, regional and industrial policies aimed at increasing productivity levels in NI.

"Furthermore, presuming that the UK has left the EU by that stage, Irish re-unification will also involve Northern Ireland re-entering the EU, which opens the possibility of EU involvement in the transition process. In summary, it is extremely difficult to be definitive around the costs of re-unification to the RoI tax payer, as this will be dependent upon a number of unknowns including negotiations around debt interest, the length of any transition period, the relative role and contributions of the UK, RoI and EU in managing such a transition and the success of any policies aimed at improving Northern Ireland productivity levels."

McGuinness and Bergin also address the issue of the UK government's subvention for Northern Ireland. They point out that historically, Northern Ireland was a net contributor to the UK's Treasury. From the 1930s, a subvention became a permanent feature of the relationship, growing (at 2014 prices) from £1bn a year in 1966 to more than £11bn in 2009/10, before falling back again.

The authors comment: "The view that in the event of a united Ireland that the total level of current subvention would become an overnight liability for the Irish tax payer is challengeable on two grounds. Firstly, subvention requirements are likely to fall, as there are aspects of current Northern Ireland expenditure that would no longer be relevant under a unification scenario. Specifically, non-identifiable expenditures, which are those that cannot be identified as benefiting a particular region and are more reflective of estimates of regional contributions towards UK wide expenditures, will not constitute part of the costs of administering Northern Ireland under unification. These non-identifiable expenditures include, NI's contribution to UK Defence spending which was £1,038m in 2014, debt interest, which amounted to £1,059m in 2014 and international services which totalled £284m in 2014. Non-identifiable expenditures totalled £2,381m in 2014 which equated to 26% of total subvention. Furthermore, there will undoubtedly be some loss of public sector jobs in administering functions that would no longer exist in a post-unification scenario, e.g. HMRC, which will reduce subvention costs further, although the net effect will be dependent on the success of former public sector workers finding re-employment.

"Secondly, NI's high subvention requirements largely reflect the region's low productivity levels, which, in turn, are related to issues such as poor relative human capital accumulation and a relatively low share of high value added, export orientated production. The long-term solution to the subvention issue lies in the adoption of policies aimed at raising productivity levels in Northern Ireland by addressing some of the structural issues raised in this study."

The authors conclude with the obvious recognition that the conduct of an Irish border poll must learn from the failings involved in the Brexit referendum, with clarity over what would be the practical outcome of the vote.

They add: "A key aspect of the current and future debate around a border poll relates to the potential cost of Irish unification. We conclude that it is difficult to be specific about this as it is determined by a number of unknowns including (a) the length and nature of any adjustment or transition period (b) the relative role of both governments during any transition period in addressing some of the key issues outlined above in reforming educational, industrial and regional policy (c) the relative success of such policies in raising Northern Ireland productivity levels (d) the role and significance of both the EU and USA in potentially reintegrating a post-Brexit Northern Ireland into the EU and assisting in promoting FDI to the region, and (e) the outcome of discussion on the issue of debt obligations. In addition to being the determinants of the costs of transition, these five areas also represent, in our view, some of the principle challenges for policy associated with any unification process. Other areas for consideration not discussed here include issues such as welfare entitlements, approaches to taxation etc. Following the example of the Scottish government, which provided detailed planning on the policy framework that was to be adopted across a range of areas in an independent Scotland, any border poll in Ireland should also be accompanied with detailed and accessible documentation outlining the opportunities and challenges associated with Irish unification. The documentation should also include proposals for the policies to be adopted in order achieve a successful transition."

THE HUEBNER ANALYSIS

The Huebner report, *Modelling Irish Reunification*[113], has made an important contribution to the analysis of the potential economic benefits of Irish reunification. It was widely criticised at the time of publication, primarily because although it was written by independent and respected academics, it was commissioned in the United States by supporters of Irish republicanism. However, this does not undermine the conclusions, given the author's credibility.

Huebner's report concluded that using its assumptions (which predate the Brexit vote), unification could benefit people across the island of Ireland by €1,497 per year in the year of implementation, rising to €2,810 per person per year within seven years of implementation. Most of the financial benefits would be felt in the north.

The report's reasoning included:

1 Tax harmonisation at RoI levels will be beneficial to the north. Lowering corporation tax levels to those of the Republic is likely to generate higher levels of foreign direct investment. (However, a working Northern Ireland Assembly could choose to do that without reunification).

2 Diminished trade barriers will increase trade. (Clearly this is correct in terms of trade between Northern Ireland and RoI and will be even more true post-Brexit.)

THE ADOPTION OF THE EURO IN THE NORTH WOULD BE BENEFICIAL

3 Adoption of the euro in the north would be beneficial, because the pound was over-valued at the time of the report's publication. (Sterling's post-Brexit devaluation means that the pound is no longer obviously over-valued against the euro, this point is out of date.)

4 Productivity improvements. (It is reasonable to assume that if Northern Ireland adopts the industrial strategy of the south then it will – over time – move towards the productivity levels of the south. But this could take decades. 27 years after German reunification, productivity remains lower in the east than in the west and wages remain lower. Achieving economic benefits from unification is a slow process.)

5 Political union will lead to rationalisation of the public sector in the north.

6 Fiscal transfers will become the responsibility of the Republic, not the UK.

One key finding of the report is how important borders are, in terms of disrupting trade. It explains: "Numerous studies done in a variety of settings (the US and Canada, among Canadian provinces) demonstrate that 'borders matter' to a much greater degree than most observers would expect." The return of a hard border on the island would obviously have been detrimental. The most aggressive unification scenario in the report estimates a boost in all-island GDP of €35.6bn over eight years with the north benefiting significantly more than the south.

The report concluded: "The model... suggests unification will raise GDP in Northern Ireland by €2.1bn to €2.6bn in the year the policy is implemented, depending on the extent to which Northern Ireland government expenditure is cut and the amount of FDI attracted by the new tax regime. These gains could accumulate to as much as €25.3bn in the first eight years following unification. GDP in the ROI could rise by €30m to €152m in the year of policy implementation, again subject to the same assumptions. Across the first eight years of unification, GDP gains in the ROI could rise from €10.3bn to €18.5bn. In total, Irish unification could boost all-island GDP in the first eight years by as much as €35.6bn."

As the authors of the report point out, in the case of German unification the smaller partner - East Germany - benefited the most. However, it should be noted that the benefits spread slowly – reunified Germany is still far from being an equal society, or having equivalent economic output. It should be noted that west and east Germany remain different places in terms of economic performance, social relations and political outlook.[114] Despite this, reunification can be regarded as having been a success. And it is reasonable to say that the task of German reunification was more challenging than would be the case of reuniting Ireland. The economic systems on both sides of the Irish border are broadly similar, though performing at different levels. In Germany, one jurisdiction had free market capitalism, while the other had state capitalism – involving subsidies for state run factories, for example. Since reunification, East German productivity has risen from 73% of the German average in 2000 to almost 80% by 2014.[115] This is significant, if slow, progress. Reintegration of divided countries is not easy.

SUMMARY

- Brexit has the potential to severely negatively impact the Northern Ireland economy;
- Northern Ireland has low productivity because of skill and infrastructure deficiencies;
- The Republic outperforms Northern Ireland and GB in productivity;
- Northern Ireland invests too little in universities and in vocational skill training;
- Regional policy is inadequate in both Northern Ireland and in the Republic, with excessive regional economic disparities;
- The Republic has much higher earnings than does Northern Ireland, but has a higher cost of living, so disposable incomes are comparable;
- Northern Ireland at present has a lower unemployment rate than the Republic, but the highest economic inactivity rate of any UK region;
- Northern Ireland has an unacceptably high level of early school leavers, without basic English, maths and IT skills;
- Low levels of private and public sector investment have held back productivity and earnings in Northern Ireland;
- Northern Ireland is more dependent on manufacturing and less on the private sector services sector than either GB or the Republic;
- An Irish Sea border between Northern Ireland and GB seems inevitable as a result of Brexit;
- Northern Ireland's economy will increasingly be linked to that in the Republic, with more trade conducted in euros and the potential for greater investment, improved productivity and higher incomes.

5
IRELAND AND BRITAIN PREPARE FOR UNITY

IRELAND IS a very different place than it was a century ago. It has become a world leader in developing socially liberal policies, after referendums which legalised divorce, gay marriage and women's reproductive rights. Ireland has become a nation separated from the Catholic Church and the attitude of Eamon de Valera, who "combined a radical political pragmatism with a stubborn economic and social conservatism".[116]

It is a country that today is thinking more seriously about Irish unity than it ever has in decades. "The EU needs to prepare for a united Ireland," explained then Taoiseach Enda Kenny, addressing the McGill Summer School in Glenties, Co. Donegal, in 2017. Leo Varadkar endorsed the comment, prior to himself leading the government, saying: "I share the vision of An Taoiseach that foresees a united Ireland at some point in the future, and I share his belief in how it should be achieved."[117] Then Tanaiste Simon Coveney later went further. "I am a constitutional nationalist, I would like to see a united Ireland in my lifetime. If possible, in my political lifetime."[118]

Taoiseach Varadkar added during 2019: "People who you might describe as moderate nationalists or moderate Catholics who were more or less happy with the status quo, will look more towards a united Ireland... I think increasingly you will see liberal Protestants, liberal unionists, starting to ask the question as to where they feel more at home."[119]

The attitude in the Republic for either support for Irish unity, or at least acceptance of it in principle, has been underlined by the strong support for Sinn Fein in the 2020 General Election in the south. Prior to that election, Leo Varadkar called for more Irish investment into Northern Ireland –influenced by the recognition that it is to the Irish state's benefit to have a northern neighbour that is economically successful.

The character of Brexit creates a more integrated all-island economy, which the Irish government has an interest in ensuring is successful. As a contingency measure if for no other reason, the Irish state needs to prepare for the prospect of Irish unity and the south taking political, economic and social responsibility for ensuring the whole of the island is functional.

In October 2019, Varadkar said that the Republic could join with the UK and Northern Ireland governments in investing in cross-border infrastructure such as road and rail links and in university expansion.[120] That would seem to be a clear statement of intent that the south is invested in the economic welfare of the north.

Others are concerned on a practical level of what a unity referendum might ask, and whether voters are likely to understand the implications. Senator Mark Daly of Fianna Fáil argues that the outcome of a referendum must be understood before any poll takes place. "The lesson of Brexit is this: you do not have a referendum and then tell everybody what the future looks like," he said. "You only have a referendum at the end of a long, long process where you debate all the issues. We've got to prepare, and we've got to prepare now. Events take over, and politicians forget this."[121] In other comments, Daly said: "it's a matter of record that the Dublin government has no policy to put to unionists in regard to unity. It's a clear case of failing to prepare is preparing to fail. Policy neglect rarely goes unpunished."

Several academic institutions have come together to consider what the referendum questions would be, how the electorates (north and south) would be comprised and the timing of any referendums. The Working Group on Unification Referendums on the Island of Ireland[122] is led by University College London and supported by University College Dublin, Queen's University, Trinity College Dublin and Ulster University. They will also consider what would happen if the referendum results go in opposite directions – specifically if the north voted for unity and the south voted against.

Project leader Dr Alan Renwick has observed that it may be necessary to hold four referendums – two (one in each jurisdiction) on the principle of unity and a second set of two to approve or reject the detailed terms of the arrangements.[123] Some of the debate might take place, he suggested, in a citizens' assembly, drawing on the experience of the use of an assembly in the Republic in advance of referendums on gay marriage and abortion.

Dr Renwick commented: "Different polls are showing different things, but there is a drift in the poll towards unification and Brexit is having a clear effect on driving greater support for unification, but most polls suggest there is still a majority for staying in the UK." He added the concern that consideration needs to be given to a refusal by unionists to engage in the process.

It has long been assumed that for unionists and Protestants, identity trumps everything else. But that may no longer be true in the post-Brexit environment. A paper on British identity in Ireland by Miceal Canavan and Oguzhan Turkoglu asserts, based on research findings: "for Protestants who experienced the conflict, there is a permanent distance between identities and switching from British toward Irish is not likely. Conversely, for people who did not experience the conflict, identities are more malleable and moving from British to Irish identity is possible.... Among Protestants who did not experience the conflict, there is a significant shift in national identity. The percentage of people who define themselves as British not Irish drops by more than 20% after the referendum. Among older Protestants, there is no significant change in identification as there is a 'permanent distance' between the identities due to their experience of violent intergroup conflict."[124]

An equally relevant point is made by Katy Hayward and Cathal McManus of Queen's University. They write: "Since 2006, according to the Northern Ireland Life and Times Survey, the largest portion of people in Northern Ireland identify themselves as neither unionist nor nationalist but as 'neither'. This fact is difficult to tally with the patterns of polarised election results and the narratives of a 'culture war' that dominate most analyses of contemporary Northern Ireland."[125] The Good Friday Agreement fails to recognise the 'neither' category, nor the proposition that a significant part of the Northern Ireland population regard themselves as both British and Irish.

In a separate article, Katy Hayward said: "It is increasingly the case that people from all backgrounds in Northern Ireland think that Brexit makes Irish unity more likely. In 2016, 18% of unionists respondents thought Brexit made a united Ireland more likely. By 2018 it was 28%. The proportion of nationalists thinking this rose from 38% in 2016 to 64% in 2018. But there is a big difference between expecting something and welcoming it. By late 2018 (the latest data we have) one in three DUP supporters said Brexit makes them even less in favour of a united Ireland. Unsurprisingly, one in two of Sinn Féin supporters said Brexit made them even more in favour of it."[126]

Professor John Garry, also of Queen's, has said that surveys of attitudes are beginning to show that many unionists while against unity if faced with it would, on reflection, prefer a 32 county administration than devolved government. Their argument is there would be no point in having failed devolution within the island and would prefer a seat at the centre of power than a place in a regional assembly.[127]

Moreover, it has been claimed that some unionists believe that there is no point in Stormont existing if (as is the case now) there is no unionist majority.

Peter Robinson is one Northern Ireland politician who has not ignored the changes that are happening in northern society. In an opinion article published in the Belfast Telegraph, he warned unionists not to take their affiliation to the United Kingdom for granted. "I do not believe calling a referendum would be justified and I have never called for it - indeed I have argued how distracting and destabilising it would be - but no amount of grandstanding changes the fact that unionists cannot stop it happening," he warned. "What I have sought is that unionists should be actively getting the rules and procedures concerning the conducting of a border poll and its aftermath sorted out to their satisfaction – now."[128]

Increasingly, politicians are also considering the possibility that demographic change, political evolution in the south and the likely impact of Brexit has meant that it has become conceivable that voters in Northern Ireland might within the foreseeable future support Irish reunification. Many in Britain would not object to this. Kevin Meagher is a former special advisor to Labour secretary of state for Northern Ireland, Shaun Woodward, and author of *A United Ireland: why unification is inevitable and how it will come about*. He wrote: "Bluntly, Northern Ireland, with a population of just 1.8 million people, is of no strategic economic importance to Britain, representing just 2% of the UK's GDP. Northern Ireland's best bet, economically, is to join with the South and align its economy to benefit from the Republic's strong record of attracting foreign direct investment."[129]

UK governments have been more equivocal, and inconsistent, about their strategic interest in terms of Northern Ireland. In 1990, the then secretary of state for Northern Ireland Peter Brooke said that "the British Government has no selfish strategic or economic interest in Northern Ireland". This position was reaffirmed by John Major as prime minister in 1993 in the Downing Street Declaration, when he again made clear "on the behalf of the British Government, that they have no selfish strategic or economic interest in Northern Ireland."[130] The statement was supported by the then leader of the opposition, Tony Blair, who carried the policy into government, which was implemented as part of the understanding behind the Belfast Agreement (Good Friday Agreement).

Theresa May while prime minister shifted government policy away from neutrality, influenced by her reliance on DUP votes at a time when she did not have a majority. In the event of a border poll, said May, a government led by her would argue for Northern Ireland remaining part of the UK. "I believe in the partnership of our four great nations in one proud Union and I want it to endure for generations to come. So a government I lead will never be neutral in our support for the Union. We will always make the case for it."[131]

Boris Johnson may have reverted to the more neutral position – though it is never clear what, if anything, the prime minister genuinely believes. And it is certainly true that Northern Ireland has proven a barrier to him in achieving the type of Brexit – outside the Customs Union and Single Market – that he demanded.

Leading Conservatives are now beginning to think what was once unthinkable. Former Conservative MP and now Times columnist Matthew Parris wrote: "Faster than many realise, the time is coming to think dispassionately about the unification of Ireland. When the expected border with the rest of the UK is established in the Irish Sea the case for reuniting north and south will get its biggest boost since partition in 1921. I suggest this may not be a bad thing."[132]

Parris added that Northern Ireland has been "a bottomless pit", in terms of UK subsidy. "It isn't working. Not far south of Belfast, in the Republic, it is." The economic measures of the Republic would transform the outlook for the north, Parris suggests.

Many people believe that the mood is shifting amongst what might be regarded as 'soft unionism'. Tony Blair's close advisor Jonathan Powell commented: "You do hear stories of middle-class unionists in the golf and the rugby clubs saying 'if we're going to leave the EU, we might as well stay in as a United Ireland'. Friends of mine tell me they're hearing this. You'd have never have heard that before."[133]

In an interview with the BBC at the end of 2019, Powell went further, saying: "Once you put a border between Northern Ireland and the rest of the United Kingdom, Northern Ireland's going to be part of a united Ireland for economic purposes. That will increase the tendency toward a united Ireland for political reasons, too. I think there is a good chance there will be a united Ireland within 10 years."[134]

Ever since the foundation of the Irish state, consideration has been given to reunification. And it was recognised that an eventual settlement may need to involve some type of devolution or federation. In 1921 Eamon de Valera declared: "We are ready to give such local autonomy to Ulster...as would be practicable, if it would make for the contentment and satisfaction of the residents there."

But there has also been a recognition that change could only happen gradually and when the circumstances meant that it made sense. Rostrevor-born T.K. Whitaker was the top civil servant in the Republic when the Troubles broke out in 1968. He advised then Taoiseach, Jack Lynch, to adopt a policy of "patience, understanding and forbearance" when dealing with unionism. Whitaker told Lynch: "The most forceful argument in favour of the patient good neighbour policy aimed at ultimate 'agreement in Ireland between Irishmen' is that no other policy has any prospect of success."

The SDLP's former leader Mark Durkan has thought carefully about how reunification might happen and the type of compromises politicians in the south might need to make to keep unionists in the north satisfied and engaged in the reformed state. The legislature and other institutions of the state would have to change under reunification. Durkan predicts that "a new dynamic would be created by the scale of northern representation in an all-Ireland parliament as compared with Westminster. That would include a substantive unionist presence."[135]

DEMOGRAPHY

Ireland has benefited massively from inward investment and from inward migration. A nation that for generations sent many of its brightest and most innovative citizens abroad to earn their living, has become a receiver of migrant workers. That process went into reverse as a result of the 2008 global financial crash – as an open market economy, which failed to properly regulate its banks and property sector, Ireland was more damaged by the international recession than most countries. Accordingly, many Irish citizens left to find work elsewhere. Since then, that process has gone into reverse, with rapidly decreasing unemployment, rising wages and net inward migration. (Ireland returned to being a country with net inward migration in 2016.[136])

The influx of young workers from across the European Union has influenced the culture of Ireland. Dublin, Cork and Galway are open minded, youthful cities, that embrace the cultures of incomers, while retaining their Irish character. There are few of the signs of racism that infest parts of England. Increasingly since Ireland joined the European Union in 1973, Ireland has become enthusiastically European. That European identity has marked the country as more socially progressive, less influenced by the Catholic Church, yet also increasingly different from its northern neighbour. For those citizens of Northern Ireland who are uncomfortable with the socially conservative and religiously

THE INFLUX OF YOUNG WORKERS FROM ACROSS THE EUROPEAN UNION HAS INFLUENCED THE CULTURE OF IRELAND. **Around 11.6% of the Republic's population as at 2016 were not Irish nationals[137] while 17.3% were not born in the Republic[138]. Some 4.5% of Northern Ireland's population at the time of the last census in 2011 were neither British nor Irish.[139]**

influenced nature of its society, the Republic is now seen as a more comfortable place, ever more at ease with itself.

Both Northern Ireland and the Republic are becoming more ethnically diverse – though the south more than the north. Around 11.6% of the Republic's population as at 2016 were not Irish nationals[137] while 17.3% were not born in the Republic[138]. Some 4.5% of Northern Ireland's population at the time of the last census in 2011 were neither British nor Irish.[139]

As a result of legislation passed in the UK Parliament, same sex marriage has been legalised, as has abortion. This brings the legal situation in the north and the south to a similar position (though at the time of writing, abortion is available later in the term in the north than in the south – but this may change).

SOCIAL REFORM

Divorce reform was one of the early examples of the Irish state's determination to modernise institutions and policies. An initial referendum proposal to permit divorce was defeated in 1986. Ireland became the only country in Europe where divorce was not possible.[140] The then Taoiseach John Bruton argued unsuccessfully that divorce reform was necessary, to demonstrate that Ireland was a tolerant and socially advanced nation – and also to send a message to Northern Ireland that its neighbour was not under the control of the Catholic Church.[141]

A second referendum in 1995 voted, narrowly, to allow for divorce, with a carefully worded proposal that made clear that divorce could not be achieved with ease and without consideration. A third referendum in 2019 further liberalised divorce law, making it easier and quicker to achieve.

Other referendums planned include potential amendments to the constitution on women's life in the home, blasphemy, reducing the voting age to 16 and extending the franchise for presidential elections to Irish citizens who live outside of the Irish state.

In 2015, Ireland became the first country in the world to hold a referendum in which the electorate voted to legalise gay marriage. Moreover – and unlike the 1995 referendum to liberalise divorce – the vote was decisive. Some 62% of voters supported legalisation, with just 38% against. This was despite the Catholic Church campaigning for a 'no' vote. "The huge 'yes' vote marks another milestone in Ireland's journey towards a more liberal, secular society," remarked The Guardian[142]. Then Taoiseach Enda Kenny said: "With today's vote we have disclosed who we are. We are a generous, compassionate, bold and joyful people who say yes to inclusion, yes to generosity, yes to love, yes to gay marriage."[143]

Ireland's onward journey to social liberalism was marked most clearly when in 2018 the country voted to reform the abortion law. The vote was even more strongly in favour of change than with gay marriage – 66.4% voted 'yes', against 33.6% for 'no'. Again, the Catholic Church campaigned, unsuccessful, for a 'no' vote. The result not only removed the equal right to life of the unborn, but also demonstrated that Ireland had transformed from a Catholic to a secular state.

Abortion is a pressing issue for the Irish health service at the time of writing, following the 'yes' vote in the referendum. Then Taoiseach Leo

Varadkar told the Dáil in June 2018 that state-funded Catholic hospitals will be required to provide abortion services. "Conscientious objection provisions will apply to individual doctors, nurses and midwives who do not want to participate in providing abortion services, but it will not be possible for publicly funded hospitals, no matter who their patron or owner is, to opt out of providing these necessary services, which will be legal in the state once the legislation is passed by the Dáil and the Seanad."[144]

A parallel process in the north took place, but only through the intervention of the UK Parliament in Westminster. It was MPs, not the Northern Ireland Assembly, that set the basis for legalisation of both same sex marriage and abortion.

HOUSING

Housing is sometimes described as Ireland's biggest policy challenge. The elements are the lag in the impact of the boom and bust of the 1990s; a shortage of available properties for affordable rent; excessive rental prices; a large number of mortgage borrowers who are unable to repay their mortgages and consequently a high proportion of non-performing loans on the books of mortgage lenders, which in turn inhibits their capacity to lend to new borrowers while also inhibiting borrowers' capacity to free up property by downsizing. Other problems include the shortage of property developers, with some put out of business by the 2008 crash and others engaged on lucrative contracts in GB.

"A survey carried out in Spring/Summer 2017 amongst 200 CEOs from across all industry sectors shows 84% of respondents see the lack of affordable housing as key challenge for business and the economy," reported Housing Europe. "Therefore insufficient housing supply is a

concern for both its economic and social reasons as the affordability of housing is deteriorating. There were 7,941 people homeless in the week of June 19- 25th 2017 across Ireland.... The phenomenon is especially concentrated in the capital. Dublin local authority homeless services are currently managing an unprecedented demand on services."[145]

While a new policy initiative, *Rebuilding Ireland - an Action Plan for Housing and Homelessness*, was launched in July 2016, there is no confidence that the housing crisis will be resolved in the near future. Housing was a key issue in the 2020 General Election. The over-stretched housing market is often cited by commentators in Northern Ireland as a factor in their hostility to reunification – though it is difficult to see how the shortage of affordable housing in Dublin would immediately or significantly affect the situation in Belfast, simply because of Irish reunification. That said, it is clear that a more effective housing policy is essential.

The combination of a booming economy, international investment, inward migration, a shortage of housing stock, enthusiastic mortgage lending and weak banking regulation proved extremely damaging to the Irish state and to mortgage borrowers when the global financial economy crashed in 2008. As yet, the Irish government has failed to address the underlying tensions that are leading to what may again be unsustainably high housing prices.

SCHOOLS

Catholic schools continue to play an important role in Ireland's education system. But the role of the Church is changing and is set to change further. Ironically, the strongest indication of that new approach came in early 2018 when then Taoiseach Leo Varadkar opened the first new Catholic school in Ireland for 30 years. He said that there would continue to be a place for Catholic schools within Ireland's state education system, but the role will decline.

He said: "There is much greater diversity now in the type of education that we offer our children and true diversity must include the catholic religion as well... While we rightly acknowledge some of the wrongs by religious congregations in the past, we should never forget the enormous good that religious congregations have done for centuries in Ireland. Setting up schools, hospitals, providing public welfare long before governments ever considered that to be part of their responsibility."[146]

Ireland's government has determined that state-funded Catholic schools can no longer discriminate against non-Catholics who seek places. Varadkar explained: "I think for a small number of schools where there is oversubscription, it is right and proper that children would not be discriminated against based on their religion. Schools are funded by the tax payer and every tax euro is equal no matter what the religion of the parents." There will be an exemption for schools of minority faiths such as the Presbyterian Church.[147]

INCOMES AND WEALTH DISTRIBUTION

Ireland performs poorly in terms of income inequality. That relative performance was largely unchanged following the global financial crash, though incomes for the poorest 10% in society have recovered better than for the richest 10% according to the OECD.[148] Ireland remains the most unequal of the OECD's 36 member states, ahead of Greece, and with the UK in fifth place, according to Nat O'Connor of Ulster University.[149] It also has the greatest gross income inequality in the EU. O'Connor observes that Ireland's income tax system is progressive at lower ends of the income scale, but that this progressivity declines at higher income levels. The tax to GDP ratio is one of the six lowest in the EU. O'Connor adds that as an essentially low tax society, Ireland inevitably has a smaller public sector and higher costs of living than other, higher taxed, states. Ireland's cost of living is 20% above the EU average.

Taxation of income on the two sides of the border is significantly different. This is a factor that could influence many people's attitudes to reunification. England and Northern Ireland personal income tax rates as at January 2020 were: income up to £12,500 is tax free; taxed at 20% from £12,501 to £37,500; 40% from £37,501 to £150,000; and 45% for income above £150,000.[150] In the Republic, income up €35,300 is taxed

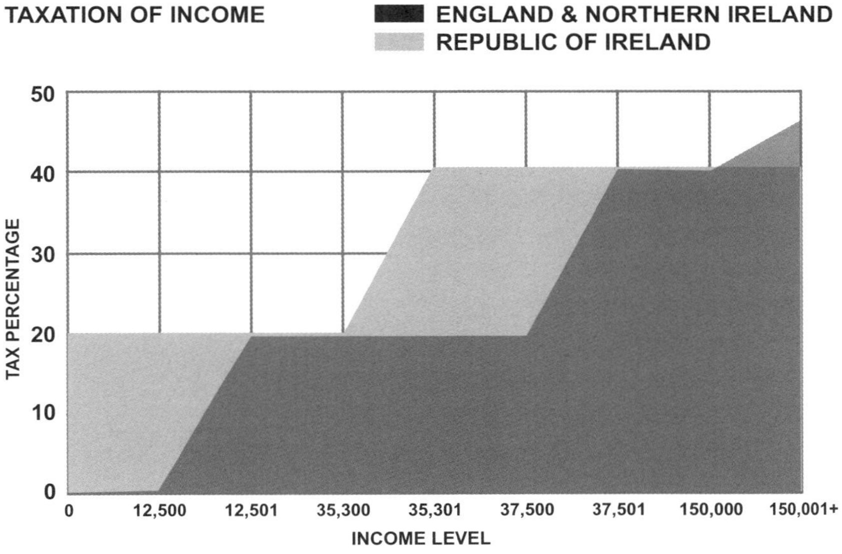

at 20%, above that at 40%. (This is for a single person without children.) The Universal Social Charge applies in addition on income at rates progressing from 0.5% to a maximum 8%. But a range of tax credits mitigate the total tax liability. Because of the complexity of the Republic's tax system it is difficult to compare the results of the two systems. Broadly, low paid workers pay less income tax in the Republic than in the UK because of the impact of the Republic's tax credits, while middle and higher income individuals pay more tax.[151] The Republic's basic corporate tax rate is 12.5%, compared to the UK's main rate of 19%. Plans to cut the UK corporation tax rate from 19% to 17%, which had been due to begin in 2020 have been put on hold.

The state pension is higher in the Republic than in the UK, but begins later. The UK's state pension is both the lowest in the EU and across the developed world.[152] However, it would for negotiation whether Northern Ireland residents would receive a UK state pension or the more generous Republic of Ireland's state pension – and which state would pay for it.

Social Justice Ireland has expressed concern at low pay in the private sector and argues that the national minimum wage is 20% below a living wage.[153]

THE DECLINE OF THE ROLE OF THE CATHOLIC CHURCH

The Catholic Church's involvement in health and schools provision in Ireland dates back to the 19th Century, at a time when the state provided neither. The role of the Catholic Church was the greater in Ireland, because such a high percentage of the population were of the Catholic faith and the British state pre-independence was regarded as being unfavourably disposed to Catholics. Following independence, the weak Eire state had insufficient funds to provide core health services and schools, and was happy to rely on the Catholic Church. In turn, the Church was able to arrange services at cheap cost through the use of members of the religious orders and volunteers.[154]

As well as being engaged in the provision of health services, the Catholic Church was also dominant in determining policy. In 1950, proposed government legislation on adoption, social welfare and support for pregnant women were all abandoned – in effect by instruction of Catholic bishops. Although the Irish constitution was secular, government was very definitely Catholic. Bishops could, and did, instruct government ministers on what to do, and more specifically what not to do.

When health minister Dr Noel Browne attempted to introduce a Mother and Child Service in 1948 that would provide free maternity care for mothers and free health care to children under 16, he was forced to leave government. The measures were abandoned. The Catholic Church had effectively vetoed them, in part because of fears that gynaecological care of pregnant women might have been provided by non-Catholics – which might have led to women being advised to have terminations, or supported in having them.

Then Taoiseach John Costello supported the Catholic bishops against his own health minister, Browne. Costello told the Dáil of his meeting with the Archbishop of Dublin, John Charles McQuaid. "I asked His Grace would he permit me to try to adjust the matter with my colleague [Browne]. His Grace readily gave me that assignment and that authority." In a subsequent letter to Browne, Costello wrote: "You are not entitled to describe your scheme as government policy and you must not so describe it hereafter unless and until you have satisfied the [Catholic] hierarchy." The Catholic Church's veto over Irish health policy was proven.[155]

Historically, unionists have argued that the Catholic grip on the Irish state was itself a strong reason for them keeping their distance, given that the majority population in Northern Ireland was attached to various forms of the Protestant religion (Presbyterian, Free Presbyterian, Church of Ireland, Methodist, Baptist and others).

Unionist attitudes to the Republic of Ireland were strongly influenced by the level of influence of the Catholic Church. Ian Paisley's words may have been stronger in criticising Catholicism than were others of his faith, but the sentiments were widely shared. Paisley described Catholism as the "Seed of the serpent." He continued: "Her clothes reek of the brimstone of the pit. Her words and opinions label her the parrot of Beelzebub, her father." He also disliked what he saw as the Catholic influence on the European Union. Paisley, long an MEP, described the EU as "A beast ridden by the harlot Catholic Church."[156]

While the Paisley prose was offensive, there were legitimate reasons for unionists and Protestants in Northern Ireland to be concerned. The incoming Irish government of 1948 sent a message, against the advice of their officials, to the Pope that they would "repose at the feet of your holiness the assurance of our filial loyalty and our devotion to your august person".

But the Republic of Ireland has gone through massive social change in recent years. The effect has not merely been that Ireland has joined the mainstream of European social liberalism, but it is one of the world's more advanced nations in terms of elements of its social policy. The Catholic Church is no longer in charge of public morality or influential over state policy. Former Taoiseach Leo Varadkar – himself gay and of mixed race – bluntly told the Pope on a visit to Ireland that the Catholic Church had been responsible for much wrong-doing in Ireland and around the world.

"This is a shared history of sorrow and shame", said Varadkar. "In place of Christian charity, forgiveness and compassion, far too often there was judgement, severity and cruelty, in particular, towards women and children and those on the margins."

In an interview, Varadkar added: "I think in the past the Catholic Church had too much of a dominant place in our society. I think it still has a place in our society but not one that determines public policy or determines our laws... We do have a Church/state dialogue that involves other churches as well and faiths other than Christian faiths too."[157]

It was one more step on a journey in which the Irish state has increasingly distanced itself from the Catholic Church.

6
SLÁINTECARE

ONE OF the essential prerequisites – arguably the most important – for obtaining greater support for Irish reunification is the establishment of a free at point of need healthcare system in the Republic of Ireland. This might be modelled on the National Health Service – but an effective NHS, not the one in Northern Ireland that is currently blighted by inadequate funding, the failure to implement reform as spelt out by the Bengoa report (and other studies) and with excessive waiting lists and waiting times.

Nor is it acceptable to residents of the north to have a system dominated by provision involving the Catholic Church. But despite the history, reform of the south's healthcare system is coming.

Inequality in the delivery of healthcare in Ireland is a serious problem, which is related to the flawed system operating in the Republic. "Those with a lower social position are more likely to report unmet health care needs, as well as unmet medical examination and treatment needs," says the Nevin Economic Research Institute. "When looking at the situation for Ireland as a whole it is clear that cost and waiting lists were the key reasons for unmet health care need, these issues are more problematic for those with lower income and lower levels of education attainment."[158]

The National Health Service in Northern Ireland is free at point of delivery – including for GP consultations and prescriptions – but is struggling to function. The Pivotal think-tank reported: "The system faces a growing financial crisis, while waiting lists are unacceptable and keep getting longer. In March [2019], there were 1,154 people waiting over a year for planned care in England. In Wales that number was 4,176. In Northern Ireland, it was 120,201."[159]

The Bengoa report proposed substantial reforms to the NHS system in Northern Ireland, essentially investing in services rather than buildings. Too much of the NHS in the north is based in old buildings, too much of it in Belfast, too little is devolved and it has too few staff or investment in specialist services. To make matters worse, Brexit is poised to further damage the service by encouraging EU26 workers to leave, while discouraging others to come to take their place.

It is essential that substantial reform of the NHS in Northern Ireland takes place, in line with the Bengoa proposals. If necessary to achieve political cover for contentious decisions, a citizens' assembly could be convened to consider the crisis in the NHS and propose solutions based on expert testimony. But one way or another, reform is essential.

The Republic's health system is also under pressure. It is over-expensive for the quality of healthcare provided. That cost is to a large extent the result of the insurance-based system used, which means that the Republic has one of the EU's highest costs for healthcare per person in the EU, without a related quality outcome.[160] The adoption of SláinteCare needs to be guaranteed through a legislative framework and legally enforceable timetable.

The McGuinness/Bergin report observes "With regard to the relative strengths of the health systems in Northern Ireland and the Republic of

Ireland, this is likely to be a key feature of any border poll debate as it is often claimed by commentators that losing access to the UK National Health Service will be a key factor preventing voters in Northern Ireland from supporting a united Ireland.

"However, our analysis suggests that the gap between the Irish and UK health systems has narrowed, presumably as a consequence of much higher levels of per capita health expenditure by the Irish government and the impacts of austerity policies in the UK. We find that the Irish system does have more up-front charges; however, it also contains balances to ensure that healthcare remains free at the point of use for the most vulnerable in society.

"Using data from the *OECD Healthcare at a Glance* report, we show hospital care coverage is substantially superior in the UK, while Ireland has somewhat higher rates of doctors, nurses, hospital beds and hospital discharges per 10,000 population. Both health systems appear to be outlying poor performers among OECD countries in terms of acute care bed occupancy rates, indicating that neither health service has enough spare capacity to deal with seasonal fluctuations in demand. A high acute bed occupancy rate is also consistent with ineffective processes for moving patients efficiently through the hospital system, which also points towards serious shortfalls in social care provision within both health systems."

A review in the Oireachtas in 2017 of the Irish health system recognised the need for change, moving closer to the UK's NHS. It proposed SláinteCare, with implementation to be achieved via a ten year programme. That implementation is behind schedule, but its adoption in full is needed as part of a programme of Irish integration.

Fine Gael entered government in 2016 with a commitment to make GP consultations for all children and youths up to age 18 free during the term of government. However, this promise was not achieved because of budgetary pressures and prioritisation of other policies. Instead, free GP consultations are being extended gradually, and will include those under age eight from September 2020. They are also free for those over 70. It is essential for the SláinteCare programme implementation to be speeded up, both to improve service provision for residents in the south and to facilitate Irish unification.

There are substantial opportunities to improve health service provision and reduce overheads by amalgamating the two health systems into a single integrated health service. Examples that have already been implemented include the all-island children's heart surgery unit in Dublin and the cross-border cancer care facility at Derry's Altnagelvin hospital. Ambulances also provide emergency cross-border cover, but this has been put at risk by Brexit. (At the time of writing it is unclear whether different medicine regulations in the two jurisdictions will prevent ambulances from crossing the border from 2021.)

Waiting lists and waiting times in both jurisdictions are unacceptable at present. Brexit removes the legal right for residents of Northern Ireland and the rest of the UK to opt for treatment in other EU countries where waiting times mean they cannot get treatment within a reasonable period. Brexit also potentially removes access to free healthcare for UK visitors to EU26 countries. These factors need to be addressed, but might be resolved for Northern Ireland's UK citizens by Irish reunification. (The Irish government has promised to underwrite the arrangement for Irish citizens living in Northern Ireland following Brexit.[161]) Social care is another area of crisis in NI, which requires public finance investment and greater integration with the health sector.

Mental health is one of Northern Ireland's most serious crises. The Pivotal think-tank reports: "Northern Ireland has the highest rates of poor mental health in the UK, but devotes a small fraction of health spending to the issue....Northern Ireland spends just 5% of its total health budget on mental health, which is less than half of the proportion allocated in England, despite estimates of local mental health problems being 25% higher than in England. The system is creaking, including in child and adolescent mental health services. Under-funding is clearly an issue but reform is also needed - on increased support for early intervention and prevention, on responsive and informed primary care, on updated facilities, and on a consistent and skilled workforce. Improving services is vital not only for our health and wellbeing but also because of the knock-on.... Health and social care effects of poor mental health on education, employment and justice issues."

The *Suicide Statistics Report*[162] from Samaritans provide the details of the crisis in Northern Ireland and places it in context with the situation in the Republic. For men, there are 28 suicides per 100,000 population in Northern Ireland, compared to 15.9 in England and 11.7 in the Republic. For women the rates are 9.5 per 100,000 in Northern Ireland, compared to 4.9 in England and 2.9 in the Republic. There is very strong evidence for the need to reform the levels of support in Northern Ireland, requiring more support and greater use of counselling and talking therapies.

A committee of the Oireachtas has proposed in its SláinteCare report[163] fundamental reform of healthcare provision in Ireland. The adoption of the committee's recommendations would be the basis for meeting many of the concerns of residents in Northern Ireland in relation to healthcare provision in a reunified Ireland. The committee reported in May 2017 and made far reaching and comprehensive proposals for the reform of healthcare in Ireland.

The starting point for the committee's approach was a recognition of weaknesses in the existing system. These included the severe pressures on the current provision; unacceptable waiting times for public patients; and poor outcomes in relation to the cost of the provision. (Ireland spends around 40% more than the EU per capita average on healthcare, yet is the only country in Western Europe not to have a universal primary healthcare system. About 70% of Ireland's healthcare spending is publicly funded, which is much less than the EU average.[164]) The committee concluded that there needs to be a universal single tier service in which patients are treated on the basis of health need rather than on ability to pay. It also concluded that better health outcomes and value for money can be achieved by re-orientating the model of care towards primary and community care. It proposed a ten year plan for health service reform, urging a political consensus be formed behind the recommendations.

Healthcare cannot be provided on the cheap and the committee was clear that resource allocation must increase, proposing an additional €233m over the period 2017 to 2027. Charges for healthcare should removed or reduced, including the removal in full of charges for emergency care by year eight. Primary care should be made universal and its services expanded, including through the provision of community-based diagnostics, with more care currently provided by the acute sector transferred to primary care providers. There should be an expansion in the public psychology service.

Other weaknesses in the current provision need to be addressed, said the committee. These include social care, with the provision made available of universal palliative care, additional services for people with disabilities and improved mental healthcare. Dentistry services also need expansion. Private activity in public hospitals was another concern of the report. Reforms need to be backed by new legislation, additional funding, political consensus and structural change, said the committee.

The funding for improved healthcare assumes allocation from Ireland's 'fiscal space'. It should be noted that this would be a competing demand for tax revenues with any continuing fiscal transfers (subvention) from the new Irish state to Northern Ireland that might be needed following unity. Funding would also need to come from higher tax revenues, not all of which are likely to be generated from increased economic activity. As NERI observes, while many individuals would need to pay more in tax, this will be partially or fully offset for many by lower private insurance premiums.[165]

SláinteCare was raised in the recent Irish general election as an important issue by the Social Democrats, who said that its full implementation would be a 'red line' for their involvement in government. The Irish Labour Party made a similar point, while Sinn Féin and the Greens made clear their commitment to SláinteCare. But there are concerns over the extent of the commitment by the main two parties – Fine Gael and Fianna Fáil – to SláinteCare.[166] However, Fine Gael promised to extend free visits to GPs to under 13s (a lesser commitment than that made in its manifesto for the 2016 general election).

The last Fine Gael government did make some progress towards SláinteCare implementation, with its imposition of new contracts for consultants. During 2020 new contracts for consultants were due to end their ability to undertake private work alongside public health service activities.[167] Outgoing health minister Simon Harris predicted that SláinteCare reform implementation would be completed ahead of schedule and will be fully in place by 2030.[168]

7
THE PROTESTANT EXPERIENCE OF IRELAND

OCCASIONALLY COMMENTATORS refer to the difficulties of Northern Ireland integrating with the Republic of Ireland because of the Catholic culture in the Republic. While this objection was fair in the past, it is surely no longer true or fair.

The referendum outcomes to legalise same sex marriage and abortion demonstrates the extent to which the Catholic Church no longer has a hold on the Republic. Instead, Ireland has become one of the most pluralist and diverse societies in Europe. It is one in which many Protestants thrive and in which the Church of Ireland and the Presbyterian Church have a strong presence.

As at 2016, 78.3% of the population of the Irish Republic were nominally of the Catholic faith.[169] (In 1961, Catholics comprised 94.9% of the Irish population.) Those who designated themselves as of no religion in 2016 made up 9.8% of the population, a sharp rise from the 5.9% who did so just five years earlier.[170] They comprise the second largest group in terms of religious designation. The next largest religious affiliations, in order, were the Church of Ireland, Muslims and the Orthodox Church.[171]

In parts of Ireland, there is a strong and practical relationship of mutual support and co-operation between the Catholic Church and the Church of Ireland,[172] which face similar demographic challenges of an ageing worshipper base and growth in religious scepticism.

Religious diversity in Ireland includes a former Taoiseach whose father is Hindu. As at April 2016, 17.3% of the residents of Ireland had been born outside the country.[173] The most common country of birth outside of Ireland was Poland, followed by the UK, with the fastest growing migration being from Romania.[174]

It would be difficult to argue that there is any impediment to advancement within Irish society today as a result of being a Protestant. In 1993, Erskine Childers became the second Protestant President of Ireland – the son of an executed republican during the Irish Civil War, who was also a Protestant. Another recent President, Mary Robinson, was a descendant of Anglo-Norman settlers: some of her family were Church of Ireland worshipers and her husband is a Protestant.

The very first President of Ireland was Douglas Hyde, another Protestant.[175] Two heroes of Irish history – Wolfe Tone and Charles Parnell – were Protestant, as were several 20th Century leaders of Irish independence, including Constance Markievicz.

Other Irish icons Sam Maguire and Sean O'Casey were from Protestant backgrounds. Prominent Protestants in Irish society today include government minister Heather Humphreys and Senator David Norris. The Monaghan village of Drum and the Donegal seaside resort of Rossnowlagh are both locations for annual Orange parades. The Irish Senate membership now includes Ian Marshall, who lives in Northern Ireland, is a Protestant and a former leader of the Ulster Farmers Union.

Andy Pollak, the former Irish Times religious affairs correspondent, commented in 2015 "the Republic of Ireland is a good place for Protestants. In the words of former Labour Party leader, Ruairi Quinn, Ireland is now a post-Catholic pluralist republic." He added: "Irish Catholicism is itself becoming more Protestant with far more emphasis on liberty of the individual conscience and participation by grass roots members than in the previously authoritarian institutional church."[176]

Moreover, the Irish government has gone out of its way to be generous to Protestant religions. The Church of Ireland former Bishop of Derry and Raphoe – a cross-border diocese – Ken Good has said that the Department for Foreign Affairs has provided the Church with significant financial support.[177]

Pollak believes that the late Garret FitzGerald's view has been confirmed that Irish society has changed more rapidly than any other society in Western Europe in recent times.

8
WHAT DOES NORTHERN IRELAND COST?

NORTHERN IRELAND does not cover its own costs. That much is indisputable. How much it costs, though, is disputed.

According to official UK government figures, public spending per head of population in Northern Ireland is greater than in any other region of the UK. In Northern Ireland it was £11,590 per person in 2018/19, which is 21% above the UK average.[178] Expenditure was lowest in the south east of England and the east Midlands. London is in effect subsidising most of the UK, with growing irritation in much of England about the cost of those regions and nations that receive subsidies.

Government spend on Northern Ireland was £21.8bn in 2018/19[179] (and is set to rise by about £2bn for the 2020/21 year, following the New Decade New Approach[180] settlement). This is not the figure for net cost to the UK Exchequer, as it does not take into account tax revenues raised in Northern Ireland. Total public revenues for Northern Ireland in the 2018/19 fiscal year were around £12.2bn.[181] This suggests the net subvention for 2018/19 was officially £9.6bn.

By comparison, the official figure for 2013/14 was £9.2bn, according to the former Northern Ireland Department of Finance and Personnel, which estimated total revenues for Northern Ireland of £14.9bn and public spending of £24.1bn.[182]

But these figures include a number of notional expenditure allocations which are not specific to Northern Ireland. If Northern Ireland were to become part of a new united Ireland, it would need to be negotiated which of these costs would be transferred to the new state. Those notional costs include debt interest, the armed forces and the royal family. NERI – the Nevin Economic Research Institute – estimated that if various non-Northern Ireland items of expenditure are removed from the figures – these are referred to as 'non-identifiable spending' – then the actual subvention for the 2013/14 year was around £5.2bn.

Tom Healy of NERI explains: "the DFP report estimates a total government revenue of £14.9bn in 2013-14 compared to a total of £24.1bn in public spending. However, when 'non-identifiable' spending is excluded total spending came to £20.1bn. So, depending on which measure of spending is used, the 'net fiscal deficit', in 2013-14 was £9.2bn or £5.2bn."[183]

Tom adds a warning note about trying to calculate future costs and benefits. He says: "Advocates of a united Ireland frequently use economic arguments to make the case for unity on the grounds that an island economy would benefit from integration and lowering of costs and inefficiencies associated with two separate jurisdictions and currency areas, etc. There is some truth in this claim (although difficult to assess because it is a very hypothetical one). It is also the case that Northern Ireland benefits from integration in to a single large UK market while both Ireland the UK benefit from partial integration into a much larger market of 500 million in the European Union." (This was written before Brexit.)

But there are other questions to consider. Which state has the legal and moral liabilities for the state pensions of UK citizens? And would the same obligations apply to retired employees of the UK state and other public bodies who live in Northern Ireland? As the UK pays pensions to UK citizens who retire to Spain or the Republic, for example, would the same principle apply to UK citizens who enter retirement living in Northern Ireland? And would that principle be affected by Northern Ireland becoming part of a new Irish state?

All these questions around liabilities need to be resolved by negotiation. Advocates of Irish unity will hope that the UK government will take a generous view, motivated by the long term reductions in their contributions to the cost of Northern Ireland. It would be helpful for university research to consider these liabilities from a legal and ethical basis, examining also any historic precedents.

Seamus McGuinness and Adele Bergin of ESRI provide a broader perspective to the debate. "A key aspect of the current and future debate around a border poll relates to the potential cost of Irish unification," they wrote. "We conclude that it is difficult to be specific about this as it is determined by a number of unknowns including (a) the length and nature of any adjustment or transition period (b) the relative role of both governments during any transition period in addressing some of the key issues outlined above in reforming educational, industrial and regional policy (c) the relative success of such policies in raising Northern Ireland productivity levels (d) the role and significance of both the EU and USA in potentially reintegrating a post-Brexit Northern Ireland into the EU and assisting in promoting FDI to the region, and (e) the outcome of discussion on the issue of debt obligations. In addition to being the determinants of the costs of transition, these five areas also represent, in our view, some of the principle challenges for policy associated with any unification process. Other areas for consideration not discussed here include issues such as welfare entitlements, approaches to taxation etc."

A much more negative assessment was put forward by John FitzGerald and Edgar Morgenroth in their report *The Northern Ireland Economy:*

Problems and Prospects[184], published by Trinity College Dublin. In this the authors quote ONS figures for 2016, indicating a deficit of £9.347bn, based on expenditure of £26.015bn and revenues of £16.668bn. They argue that one distortion included in the ONS figures is the calculation of the distribution of corporation tax revenues, with Northern Ireland being notionally allocated less of the tax revenues than it actually generates. If these revenues were more accurately allocated to Northern Ireland, then this would increase revenues by around £500m, they calculate.

FitzGerald and Morgenroth also consider the breakdown of identifiable and non-identifiable expenditure. The specific identifiable expenditure for Northern Ireland for 2016 is shown as £20.562bn. If the deficit were adjusted to include only identifiable items and corrected with regard to corporation tax revenue allocations, this would bring the subvention down to £3.394bn. However, even within a unified Ireland, various non-identifiable costs for a new Irish state would have to be recognised in Northern Ireland.

It should be noted that FitzGerald and Morgenroth make various assumptions. Specifically, they assume "that Northern Ireland would leave the UK without accepting any liability for existing public debt". They are not taking into account any change in revenues as a result in constitutional or policy change following unification. The calculation they make does assume contributions to the broader cost of an all-island state. On this basis they calculate the potential deficit of Northern Ireland within a united Ireland of around £6.9bn (€8.4bn) a year. The figure would rise to around £8bn (€9.8bn) if Northern Ireland did have to take a share of UK public debt.

FitzGerald and Morgenroth conclude: "The best economic outcome for Northern Ireland is one where future UK governments commit to providing continuing large transfers to Northern Ireland for at least a further decade in return for a change in regional economic policy aimed at promoting economic growth. Public expenditure needs to be reallocated from sustaining consumption, especially public services, to investing in education and infrastructure. While painful initially, it would move the Northern Ireland economy onto a sustainable growth path. Another option, Irish unity, if it involved ending transfers to Northern

Ireland, would produce a dramatic fall in the standard of living there. Alternatively, unification, where Ireland took over responsibility for the transfers to Northern Ireland, would necessitate a major cut in the standard of living in Ireland of 5% to 10% in order to allow Northern Ireland to maintain a standard of living between 10% and 20% above the Irish standard of living. Whatever form Irish unity took there would be a heavy economic cost for both Northern Ireland and Ireland."

The reasons for the more negative projection made by FitzGerald and Morgenroth compared to my own is that the assumptions made are substantially different. Specifically, they regard only £2.1bn of the existing UK subvention to Northern Ireland as being related to non-NI items, compared to the £5bn or so as calculated by Tom Healy. This significant difference suggests the need for more detailed work to reach an agreed calculation on the real level of UK subvention to NI, based on actual Northern Ireland costs.

However, the central difference between the assumptions made by FitzGerald and Morgenroth and myself is whether a period of transition takes place. My working assumption is that we need a ten year (or similar) period of transition, during which Northern Ireland's weak economy is corrected to substantially reduce the fiscal deficit. McGuinness and Bergin make a similar working assumption. The assumption by FitzGerald and Morgenroth is of what is in effect a 'big bang' transfer, with little or nothing done in advance of the constitutional change to correct the weak economic and social situation of Northern Ireland. Therefore, while the terminology and tone is different, the substance of the FitzGerald and Morgenroth argument is consistent with the approach advocated in this book.

Ulster University economist – and former Ulster Unionist Party MLA – Esmond Birnie responded to the FitzGerald and Morgenroth report in comments to the Belfast News Letter[185]. He said that whatever economic approach is taken to unification would be "problematic", given the subvention, which he quoted at around £10bn.

"A case can be made that post-unity a Dublin government would not need to make quite so large a transfer," Birnie said, accepting that if collective costs such as those relating to defence and diplomacy are removed the figure might be argued to be around £6bn. Even this, he suggested, would be difficult for the Republic's tax revenues to cover, as they would represent about £1,250 per person, including children, every year. "Either they pay more taxes, borrow more or accept less money will be spent on public services within the former Republic of Ireland," he said.

Birnie added that was no guarantee that the UK state would agree to phase out the subvention over a period of transition. The News Letter quoted him saying: "But is that a realistic assumption?"

Senator Mark Daly has produced a much more optimistic scenario. He notes: "In July 2018 Senator Daly and Gunther Thumann[186] compiled research for the Good Friday Agreement Implementation Committee on the true income and expenditure of Northern Ireland in a reunification situation. The information analysed by Daly & Thumann shows that, in fact, the current reported deficit for the Northern Ireland budget could come close to a balanced budget in a re-unification scenario."[187]

This report drew on earlier researched (including some contained in this book), in particular that commissioned by Congressman Brendan Boyle from the United States Congressional Research Service. This earlier researched examined the income and expenditure for Northern Ireland with a view to producing an independent assessment of the actual subvention of Northern Ireland in the event of Irish reunification.

There are several important factors that led Daly and Thumann to achieve a more positive outlook. At the heart of these are a different set of assumptions in relation to the future relation between Ireland and the UK.

Northern Ireland's fiscal accounts are adjusted to bring them into line with the statistical requirements for UK government accounts. Thumann calculated that £1.1bn of the accounting adjustments would not apply to Northern Ireland in a reunification scenario. (The adjustments include the Bank of England Asset Purchase Facility, Central Government Capital Consumption, VAT refunds and imputed subsidies.) Pensions represent a vital issue.

Daly notes: "Thumann argues in his research that pensions would initially be the responsibility of the British Government as the pension liability was accrued while Northern Ireland was part of the United Kingdom." This relates to pension liabilities relating both to state retirement pensions and occupational pensions for former employees of the UK state. This constitutes identifiable expenditure in Northern Ireland's 2012-13 Social Protection budget of £2.8bn.

Thumann believe there are significant items included by the Treasury in calculating expenditure related to Northern Ireland that should not be included. Daly explains: "Non-identifiable expenditure of £2.9bn includes Northern Ireland's share of UK Defence Expenditure, UK Debt Interest, International service, UK contribution to the EU, British Royal family etc. These would not be a liability of a new agreed Ireland. Thumann in his research explains that not all the accounting adjustments figure attribute by Westminster to Northern Ireland of £1.1bn would be applicable in a reunification scenario either."

They add: "While this £9.2bn figure is a statistical measure of the 2013-2014 fiscal situation in Northern Ireland (as part of the United Kingdom) it would not be an adequate measure for the fiscal balance of Northern Ireland under a unification scenario with the Republic of Ireland. First, the Boyle report data contain expenditure items which would not be present under a unification scenario. Second, the fiscal situation of Northern Ireland will depend on the economic situation and the tax and expenditure structure at the time of unification, which could be quite different from that in 2013/14. Third, the future fiscal situation of Northern Ireland will reflect policies adopted in the context of unification."

Thumann points out that while German reunification has not achieved economic equality, it has created a substantial improvement in the east German economic situation. He wrote: "East German productivity rose rapidly in the first ten years of unification – from about 45% of the West German level in 1991 to about 75% in 2001. East German productivity was still a little below 80% of West German productivity in 2013. In 2013, disposable household income per capita in East Germany had reached €17,614, equivalent to 83% of the West German level; the gap had narrowed considerable from the 61% figure measured in 1991."

Daly and Thumann assume that unification could achieve significant savings, in particular by thinning out the north's public sector. Daly notes: "The convergence of the public service numbers between the north and the south would bring a saving of £1.7bn per annum in the current budget expenditure of Northern Ireland."

Daly concludes: "Taking the above adjustments and savings into account the cumulative figure is £8.5bn. With the reported deficit for Northern Ireland is at £9.2bn therefore the current income and expenditure figure for Northern Ireland Thumann & Daly concludes comes near a balanced budget in a reunification scenario. This is of course, before taking into account the likely potential for growth in Northern Ireland following unification as happened in East Germany following its reunification."

Huebner predicts significant increases in tax revenues following unification.

NORTHERN IRELAND'S PUBLIC SECTOR

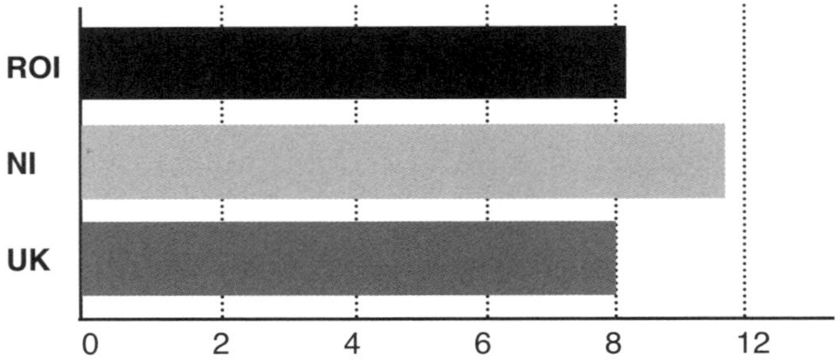

Percentage of population employed as public servants

There are around 396,100 public servants in the Republic of Ireland,[188] 8.4% of the population. There are around 206,430 public servants in Northern Ireland,[189] 11% of the population. This compares to 8% for the whole of the UK. (The statistics for RoI comprise the civil service, defence, the garda, education, regional bodies, health and semi-state companies. For Northern Ireland, the figure comprises employees of Northern Ireland central government, arm's length government bodies; UK central government employees based in Northern Ireland, local government and public corporations.)

More than 50,000 jobs would go if the public sector in the north were reduced in proportionate size to that of the Republic. Average weekly public sector pay in Northern Ireland is £623[190]: this suggests the potential annual cost savings of a loss of 50,000 public sector jobs in Northern Ireland is around £1.6bn per annum in wages, plus £145m in national insurance contributions. In addition, workplace accommodation costs would be saved. However, the loss of these jobs would potentially create additional welfare benefits costs and loss of spending in the wider economy, unless equivalent jobs could be created in the private sector. In recent years across the UK, the loss of public sector jobs has been less than the creation of new jobs in the private sector – but these have typically been at lower rates of pay and a high proportion of them have been self-employed or otherwise insecure.

While the direct cost savings to public sector bodies would potentially be in excess of £1.7bn a year, the net benefit to public expenditure would be significantly less than this. It should also be recognised that the capacity of the public sector in Northern Ireland to reduce assumes not only greater efficiency, but also that the security situation is normalised, with no increase in politically-motivated violence before or after Irish reunification.

THE ATTITUDE OF THE BRITISH

Any discussion of the prospect of a United Ireland needs to take into consideration the attitude of the population of Great Britain. Given the absence of concern for the impact of Brexit on Northern Ireland within the Brexit debate (other than within Northern Ireland), it seems reasonable to infer that it is not a major issue

for large numbers of people in Britain. Indeed a post-Brexit opinion poll suggests that the majority of the British population are indifferent to Northern Ireland.

An opinion poll survey conducted in January 2018 asked a sample of voters whether an independent trade policy was more or less important than "protecting the soft Irish border". Across the UK there was a 58% preference for an independent trade policy, compared to just 28% who prioritise a soft Irish border. Northern Ireland was the only UK region where a soft border was regarded as more important than an independent trade policy.[191]

Attitudes have hardened against Northern Ireland in recent years in parts of English society, as problems over Brexit worsened. A YouGov opinion poll found that most Conservative Party members would prefer to see Northern Ireland leave the UK than for Brexit to be abandoned. The margin was decisive, with 59% favouring a Northern Ireland breakaway, against 28% preferring to give up on Brexit. The margin for losing Scotland was even greater, with a 63%/29% split.[192]

This provides clear evidence that concerns for Northern Ireland are not prominent in the minds of the British electorate. If those British voters were given a choice as to whether to retain Northern Ireland within the UK, the answer might well depend on the issue of cost. (As far back as 2012, Kelvin McKenzie was making the argument in the Daily Telegraph that Northern Ireland and other regions should lose their subventions and live from their own resources.[193])

While there is a debate over the real level of UK government subvention to Northern Ireland, there is clarity over the much higher public spending in Northern Ireland. Public spending per head of population in 2018/19 Northern Ireland was £11,590, which is 21% above the UK average, and the highest amount of any UK region. In both the south east and east Midlands of England it was £8,601.[194] Much of this difference comes down to the much larger size of the public sector in Northern Ireland.

A major restructuring of Northern Ireland in terms of its public spending position within the UK seems likely, or inevitable, even if it continues within the UK. The removal of Northern Ireland as a cost to the UK would be welcomed by large numbers of taxpayers in GB, particularly in England. It seems very likely that whatever happens politically that there must be substantial reform in the coming years to the Northern Ireland economy and structure of public service delivery.

ADDRESSING THE SUBVENTION

Subventions – transfers of money from richer areas to poorer regions – are a normal part of government. London is always likely to be richer than Sunderland, just as Dublin is always likely to be richer than Donegal. The discovery of resources wealth – North Sea oil and gas, for example – can reverse fiscal transfers in the short term, but urban dynamos will usually come back out on top.

Consequently, the objective is not to eliminate any form of fiscal transfer or financial support from the wealthiest areas to the poorest ones. But it is a reasonable objective to avoid waste and improve economic efficiency and productivity.

Some politicians have argued that the Republic has a level of fiscal spare capacity now to cover a level of subvention to the north. However, the lingering impact of the global financial crisis and the specific impact of the banking bail-out have left the Republic with a continuing public debt of around €200bn.

There was a minute revenue surplus in the 2019 year of €50m[195], following several years of deficits. For 2020 it is predicted the government will return to deficit, at a figure of around €1bn, rising to €1.6bn in 2021.[196] This leaves precious little opportunity to accommodate a large subvention in Northern Ireland post-unity.

It can be expected that during a referendum campaign the argument will be made that given this continuing deficit that the Republic is not in a position to cover a substantial subvention in the north. In turn, this implies that opinion polling suggesting strong support in the Republic for unification might change during the course of a referendum. It also provides the obvious conclusion that there needs to be a process of transition – this book suggests ten years – in which the weak economic situation of the north be overcome through the adoption of the policy measures that have been shown to be successful in the south.

According to FitzGerald and Morgenroth, the annual subvention received by Northern Ireland is in the region of £6.9bn. Tom Healy, formerly of NERI, suggests a more accurate figure is around £5.2bn.

Sinn Féin has suggested the subvention "could be as low as £2.7bn"[197]. It argues that the subvention is distorted by the inclusion of £2.9bn on debt, armed forces and other non-NI items; £1.1bn on asset depreciation; £1.7bn on contributions to UK government departments outside NI; and £1.3bn of annually managed expenditure, that is administered according to UK political priorities, not those of devolved government in Northern Ireland.

NICVA has also considered the question of how much the subvention really is and how to calculate it accurately.[198]

It would certainly be helpful – indeed essential – to achieve agreement on the level of subvention as part of negotiations on Irish unity, in advance of the referendums. Matters to be resolved include which jurisdiction would be responsible for pension liabilities for both former UK state and public sector employees and for UK retirement pensions for residents of Northern Ireland. Research by Mark Daly has suggested a figure of £2.8bn a year would be up for negotiation regarding pension liabilities.

We also know that Northern Ireland's public sector is in dire need of reform. The Alliance Party claims[199] that between £750m and £1.5bn are wasted annually through the provision of duplicated services, based on Northern Ireland's disputed tribal history. In addition, the public sector in Northern Ireland is much larger than that in either the Republic of Ireland or England in terms of the number of public sector workers as a proportion of the population. Reducing the size of the public sector to the proportion in the Republic and England would potentially generate savings of around £1.7bn a year. That figure is consistent with those produced by the Alliance Party, given that the higher number of public sector staff in Northern Ireland are not only the result of duplicated service provision, but also the failure to introduce some productivity improvements.

In addition, it is reasonable to assume that the adoption of the Republic of Ireland's economic policies would, over time, generate significantly greater tax revenues than are current provided. In addition, by creating far more jobs they would also raise higher levels of income tax and national insurance contributions, as well as increasing consumer spending and so increase higher levels of VAT and property tax.

It would appear that there are no published studies estimating how tax revenues would vary post unification. However, we can make a rough and ready estimate. The UK exchequer at present raises around £15bn a year from taxes in Northern Ireland. With a population of 1.8 million people, that is about £8,300 per person. By comparison, tax revenues in England are more than £10,000 per person, per year.[200]

The Republic of Ireland generated tax revenues in the 2019 year of €59.3bn (£50bn), which is projected to rise to €76.8bn (£65.2bn) by 2025[201] – even after taking into account the loss of €2bn (£1.7bn) a year from changes to the global corporate tax environment caused by the BEPS process[202]. Ireland's population in 2019 was 4,921,500[203], so tax revenue per person in the Republic was €12,050, or just over £10,000 and so comparable with England.

Consequently, it would be hoped and assumed that within a decade that Northern Ireland could achieve tax revenues per person that are comparable to those in England and the Republic of Ireland. That would generate an addition £1,700 per person per year, or £3bn a year.

REMOVING THE 'ARTIFICIAL' SUBVENTION	
UK debt interest and other UK costs	£2.9bn
UK govt pension liabilities	£2.8bn
Accounting adjustments	£1.1bn
Total to be removed in calculating Northern Ireland subvention	**£6.8bn**

We can see from this table, that the nominal Northern Ireland subvention (as calculated by the UK Treasury) of £9.6bn can be reduced by around £6.8bn by stripping out UK liabilities and liabilities that will be argued during negotiations to be UK liabilities. That leaves a net Northern Ireland real subvention of around £2.8bn. Of course, it is true that Northern Ireland would have to be bear its share of the costs of the new Irish state – though these are, for the most part, existing commitments that are met by the Irish state.

It is also possible to calculate how Irish unity would enable Northern Ireland to reduce costs and increase revenues.

A 10 YEAR PROGRAMME FOR REDUCING COSTS AND INCREASING REVENUES			
YEAR	INTEGRATING PUBLIC SERVICES	INCREASE (DECREASE) IN TAX REVENUES	TOTAL REDUCTION IN SUBVENTION
1	£170m	(£150m)	**£20m**
2	£340m	zero	**£340m**
3	£510m	£150m	**£660m**
4	£680m	£450m	**£1.13bn**
5	£850m	£900m	**£1.75bn**
6	£1bn	£1.2bn	**£2.2bn**
7	£1.2bn	£1.5bn	**£2.7bn**
8	£1.4bn	£2bn	**£3.4bn**
9	£1.6bn	£2.7bn	**£4.3bn**
10	£1.7bn	£3bn	**£4.7bn**

A 10 YEAR PROGRAMME FOR REDUCING COSTS AND INCREASING REVENUES

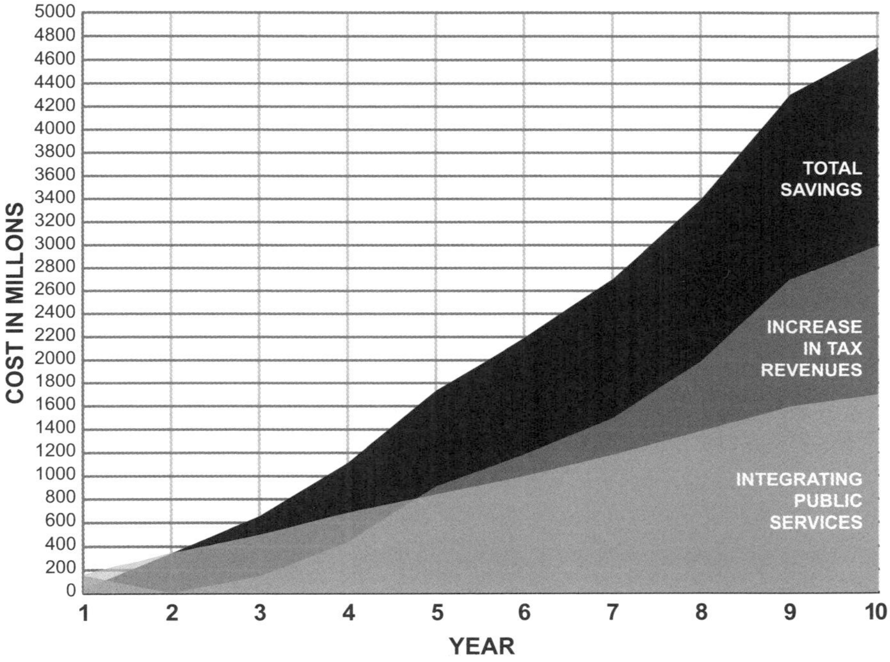

Over a 10 year period the fiscal position of Northern Ireland is improved by £4.7bn a year, which is around £1.9bn greater than the real level of current Northern Ireland subvention. This is achieved through policies that reduce the size of the public sector, pro rata, to that of the Republic of Ireland and by adopting economic policies that generate the same level of taxes, pro rata, as those of the Republic of Ireland. By these calculations, efficiency savings and improved tax revenues will more than eliminate the Northern Ireland subvention.

These outcomes are not guaranteed and might be less positive than these projections – though they might also come out better. Harmonisation of the public sector would take several years, with the maximum use of natural wastage. The process could create short term redundancy costs and unemployment and pension costs. There is no guarantee that increased tax revenues will flow as quickly as projected following unification.

9 FAILED DEVOLUTION: NORTHERN IRELAND

DEVOLUTION IN Northern Ireland has differed from that in Scotland and Wales. Firstly, the law-making powers devolved to the three devolved nations differ. Secondly, Scotland and Wales were in essence functioning places prior to devolution – and they continued to function effectively after devolution. For both Scotland and Wales devolution meant giving local politicians the power to make careful adjustments to existing programmes and spending priorities that reflected policies their parties had been elected to implement.

In Northern Ireland, the situation has been very different. Northern Ireland was not operating effectively prior to devolution. It was in crisis – a crisis in the sense that the Troubles afflicted civil society and government for 35 years. And the sectarianisation of government meant layers of excessive spending – the security forces were too big for a peaceful society and spending on schools, hospitals, housing administration and community facilities were bloated because of service duplication. The Alliance Party has estimated the cost of failing to integrate service provision at between £750m (€883m) and £1.5bn (€1.77bn) a year.[204]

Add to these inherent and inherited problems the strong mutual antipathy felt between members of some of the different parties, it was perhaps simply too much to expect a Northern Ireland Executive to emerge that could undertake fundamental reform of society and its governmental institutions. Whether that is the case or not, the truth is that devolved government has failed to achieve these reforms. The obvious example is with the NHS, where Northern Ireland has the longest waiting times and waiting lists of any UK region.[205]

Devolution has also been disappointing for Northern Ireland in terms of its economic impact. When the GFA was signed in April 1998, the Northern Ireland employment rate was 65.4%. By early 2020, this had increased to 72.6%[206]. Compare that to the UK situation. At the time of the GFA the UK employment rate was 71.7%, which increased to 76.3% in early 2020[207]. In 1998, Northern Ireland lagged the UK employment rate by 6.3%. At the beginning of 2020, it lagged it by 3.7%. This was a significant narrowing of the gap in employment performance between Northern Ireland and GB.

However, this improvement has only happened very recently – for many years the gap increased. And Northern Ireland still has an exceptionally large number of people of working age who are economically inactive. At 25.7%[208] this remained the highest rate in the UK, reflecting high levels of disability, ill health and low skill levels in parts of the population.

This performance differential has been noted by the Resolution Foundation.[209] A comparison in the reduction in the proportion of households where no one is working shows that Northern Ireland dramatically underperformed every other UK region. In the period between 1996/99 and June 2018, there was a 9.7% reduction in Northern Ireland households in which no one was working. This was the weakest improvement of any UK region, about half as good as next weakest (the East Midlands, where the improvement was 18.7%). The UK average was an improvement of 27.4%, while in Inner London the improvement was 49.3%. This represents a startling economic and social underperformance in Northern Ireland compared to every other UK region.

This has created a situation where Northern Ireland has the highest

proportion of any UK region of households in which no one is working. In NI, it is 21%[210]; the UK average is 13.5%[211].

The failure of devolution to improve the fundamental strength of Northern Ireland's economy has been noted by commentators. John FitzGerald observed: "The history of the Northern economy, since the Good Friday agreement, is that there has been little progress in transforming it into a self-sufficient economy, which could sustain the standard of living currently supported through transfers from London."[212]

Overall, devolution in Northern Ireland has been a failure in terms of economic development policy and outcomes. As the well-known Northern Ireland economist John Simpson has observed, looking at what has happened since the Good Friday Agreement and based on what has happened elsewhere, Northern Ireland should now be in a much better position. "UK and Irish comparators suggest that average personal incomes might be about 6%-8% higher, employment could be 5% higher and net emigration several thousand lower."[213]

As well as reflecting a failure in government leadership within Northern Ireland, there is also a clear failure in leadership by the UK government, spanning several political generations. This has resulted in a very high level of inequality within the UK. (Former Greek finance minister Yanis Varoufakis argues that the pro-Brexit referendum outcome was a result of the failure of English regional economic policy.[214]) Inner London is the richest region in Northern Europe[215]; by contrast Northern Ireland is one of the poorest regions in Northern Europe[216].

There has also been a massive failure by government – under direct rule and in pre- and post-Troubles devolved administration – to address sub-regional requirements. There is a large variation in productivity rates across Northern Ireland (see above), which reflects the lack of investment in skills and infrastructure outside of Belfast. It is further reflected in the substantial variation in unemployment rates across Northern Ireland. As at January 2020, the claimant count rate across Northern Ireland was 2.5%, but 4.5% in the north west (Derry City and Strabane District Council), the highest rate in Northern Ireland.

It was easier in previous years to compare local employment rates. In mid 2018, while the UK's employment rate was 75.6% and the Northern Ireland employment was 69.7%, in the Derry City & Strabane Council area the rate was 56.8%. This was almost certainly at the time the lowest employment rate for any sub-region in the UK. (Changes in the way statistics are recorded make it impossible to provide more recent, accurate, figures.) In January 2020, the Northern Ireland employment rate was still 3.7% below that of the UK rate.

At the time of writing, the Northern Ireland Executive and Assembly have just been resurrected. The New Decade New Approach agreement requires the Executive to undertake fundamental reform of Northern Ireland's institutions. We shall see if they are up to the job. Those of us who believe that the best social and economic outcome for the north of Ireland is as part of a united Ireland need to persuade others that making Northern Ireland work better is an essential part of the journey to Irish unity.

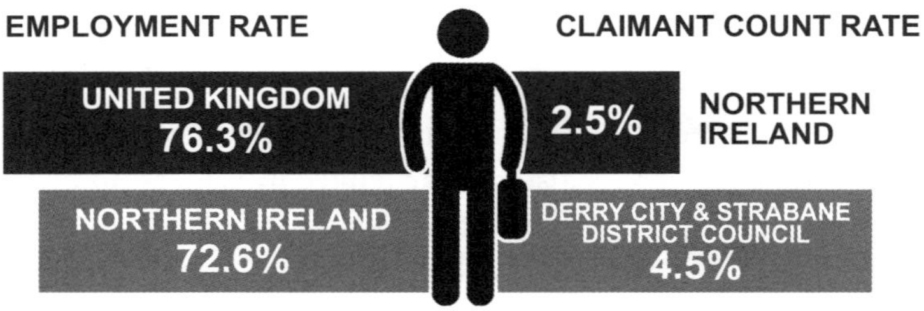

10 SUCCESSFUL DEVOLUTION: SCOTLAND

SCOTTISH INDEPENDENCE has become increasingly likely. In part, the increase in support for demands for independence has mirrored the rise of English nationalism, as illustrated by the vote for Brexit. But the calls for independence pre-date this and support has gone alongside support for the SNP and satisfaction with its performance in government. This provides a clear and strong message for Irish republicans and nationalists.

In 1999, the SNP achieved a vote of 29% in the first Scottish Parliament elections. This fell to 24% in 2003, before rising to 33% in 2007, 45% in 2011 and 47% in 2016. In terms of elections to UK Parliament, in 2019 the SNP had 54 MPs elected, out of 59 Scottish MPs (and two of the other five MPs were independents who had been SNP candidates). The SNP has also been the largest party in each of the last three regional council elections. By any measure, support for the SNP is significant and impressive and is closely correlated with satisfaction for its performance in devolved government.

The SNP has benefited politically from what it argues has been a string of achievements from its government.

THE SNP'S 19 'SUCCESSES'

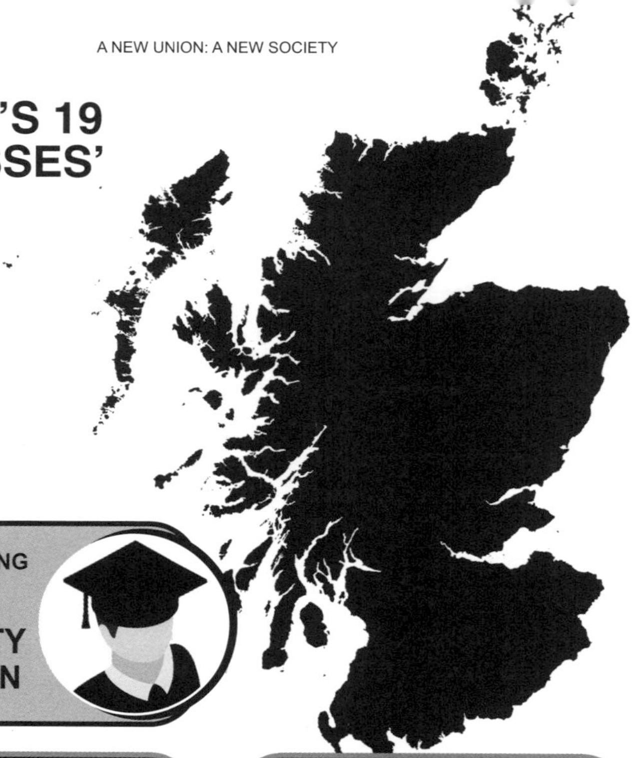

RE-INTRODUCING **FREE** UNIVERSITY EDUCATION

BUILT OR REFURBISHED **751** SCHOOLS

PROVIDED **PROPERTY RATES RELIEF** FOR SMALL FIRMS

EXTENDED THE PROVISION OF **FREE** PRE-SCHOOL CHILDCARE

INCREASED **SPENDING ON THE NHS**

COMPLETED MORE THAN **70,000** AFFORDABLE HOMES

INCREASED **NHS STAFF NUMBERS** BY MORE THAN **12,000**

ABOLISHED PRESCRIPTION CHARGES

PROVIDED 230,000 APPRENTICESHIPS

INCREASED THE NUMBER OF POLICE OFFICERS

PROVIDED 'BABY BOXES' OF PROVISIONS AT BIRTH

BANNED FRACKING

SET-UP THE SCOTTISH NATIONAL INVESTMENT BANK

INTRODUCED SAME SEX MARRIAGE

CONTINUED THE PROVISION OF FREE SOCIAL CARE FOR THE ELDERLY

CONTINUED THE PROVISION OF FREE BUS PASSES FOR THE ELDERLY/ DISABLED

ABOLISHED TOLLS ON THE FORTH BRIDGE AND TAY BRIDGE

BUILT THE QUEENSFERRY CROSSING

BUILT THE BORDERS RAILWAY

Some of these claims are regarded by critics as excessive, for example a previous government made the commitment to the Borders Railway, but construction began and completion achieved under SNP administration. What is important, though, is that the SNP can legitimately claim credit for a sustained period of administrative competence, political leadership and policy delivery. That has not only provided continued electoral support for the SNP, but also provided a strong baseline for its increasingly popular campaign for Scottish independence.

By contrast, there are many republicans who believe that the failure of the northern state provides a strong justification for Irish unity. One leading political representative of Sinn Féin said at a public meeting in 2019 (speaking alongside the author) that there was “no way” they would ever try to make Northern Ireland work.

It has been argued that a referendum for Irish unity will follow a successful vote for Scottish independence. However, Boris Johnson has responded that he will not agree to a referendum during this Parliament – which could last until 2024. It is likely that legal action may be required to bring about an earlier referendum on Scottish independence. The same situation could apply in Northern Ireland.

However, the evidence is clear from experience in Scotland that Irish unity referendum support would grow from demonstrating sustained competence in government in Northern Ireland. Not only would that show voters in Northern Ireland that nationalists and republicans can be trusted as political leaders, but also show voters in the Republic that they will not be required upon reunification to resolve all the economic and social legacy problems. Indeed, it is very likely that Sinn Féin would not have achieved their impressive Irish General Election result in 2020 had they not returned to government in Northern Ireland shortly before.

Those who want Irish unity would be best served by making Northern Ireland work. This would improve their credibility, while reducing the burden faced by the government of a newly united jurisdiction.

11
VIEWPOINTS ON IRELAND'S FUTURE

WHETHER IN the foreseeable future Northern Ireland decides to become part of a united Ireland, or whether it continues as part of the UK, there must be a similar path to progress. A Northern Ireland that is a devolved part of the UK must achieve proper, generous reconciliation between different identities. This is equally true – arguably even more so – should Northern Ireland become part of a reunified Ireland.

The Good Friday Agreement was intended as the basis for creating a shared society, in which communities became integrated and reconciled. They would move on from the past. There was an expectation that there would be a peace dividend, which would create jobs and higher incomes. The failure of that ambition is illustrated by the continuing large gap between the employment rate (the percentage of working age adults in employment) in Northern Ireland and the rest of the UK. Northern Ireland has not caught up with Great Britain economically in the past 20 plus years, despite expectations and initial optimism after the GFA.

We need to radically and fundamentally reform Northern Ireland's institutions. As the former chair of the Parades Commission and the Community Relations Council Peter Osborne observes: "We need to take dramatic, bold policy decisions that are going to structurally change this society.... What we need to do is tackle the causes of segregation and we haven't done that yet. I'm talking about the reconciliation agenda, about the structural change, about how we organise this society, particularly around housing and education."

Peter Sheridan of Co-operation Ireland made the interesting proposal that a Department for Reconciliation should be established by the Executive. Certainly the focus on reconciliation by the Executive has been inadequate and arguably abandoned, with a willingness instead to accept what might be regarded as 'separate development'.

In 2010, the Joseph Rowntree Foundation published *From a 'shared future' to 'cohesion, sharing and integration'*. This pointed out the damage caused by replacing the objective of reconciliation with the lesser one of cohesion. Mutual accommodation had become the aim, rather than tackling the roots and continuation of sectarianism. As one of our interviewees, lawyer Philip Gilliland, observed, voluntary segregation is not good enough. As a society, we need to heal. And that healing must encompass the whole of the island.

There is an interesting parallel here. Former deputy first minister Mark Durkan told us that one of the most regrettable reverses in the devolution process in Northern Ireland was the ending of the Civic Forum. It had been seen – particularly by the Women's Coalition – that the strengthening of civic society was an important step towards binding Northern Ireland together, while also creating a broader and more effective system of political accountability, which went beyond party politics.

In the Republic, the role of the Citizens' Assembly was hugely influential in putting forward amendments to the constitution regarding gay marriage and abortion, as well as bringing forward proposals on strengthening environmental protection. A broader civic engagement has proved to be a progressive move in the Republic, and it is to be hugely regretted that Northern Ireland has been slow to do the same – though measures in the New Decade New Approach agreement offer hope that this will happen on a limited basis.

Deputy Leader of the Alliance Party, Stephen Farry made an important observation in an interview with us, pointing out that it was the slow progress towards full implementation of the Good Friday Agreement that led to increased electoral support for the more hard line political parties. History cannot be reversed, but perhaps some elements of the Good Friday Agreement that have been abandoned should be reevaluated, such as the Civic Forum (or a possible replacement citizens' assembly).

It is to be hugely welcomed that the DUP is itself going through a period of reflection. We have included a summary of points made by former DUP finance minister Mervyn Storey, who expressed a willingness for greater compromise in future government. He was not the only senior DUP member that we spoke with and it is clear that the DUP is very aware that it must be more inclusive in government if the Executive is to work in the future. One of the points made by Mervyn Storey – and from others outside the DUP – was that he was unsure who really made decisions in Sinn Féin and this undermined trust within the Executive.

Part of the purpose of this book and our earlier reports was to ask key influencers from different backgrounds what their core values were. The hope is that if we can focus on values, rather the community identities, it might be possible to make progress. It was heartening to have engagement from almost the entire political spectrum.

A number of values were expressed repeatedly. These values were 'reconciliation', 'respect', 'honesty', 'truth', 'rule of law', 'inclusion', 'equality' and 'justice'. Significantly, almost everyone said it was essential that government must be 'future focused' and concentrate on delivering agreed outcomes. It might be hoped that establishing a government around those values might assist with progress and stability.

There were some points of disagreement. Some said that 'trust' was essential, whereas Former Sinn Féin Finance Minister, Máirtín Ó Muilleoir suggested that it was possible to have government without mutual trust, providing there was agreement. However, this is presumably the reason why Stephen Farry referred to the Executive operating in the past as having been a "transactional clearing house", with the key decisions taken outside of the room and just being rubber stamped in the Executive. It is important to stress, though, that Independent Unionist and Former Justice Minister, Claire Sugden reported that in her later period as a minister this was not her experience. While Stephen Farry felt the minority parties were not treated with respect on the Executive, Claire Sugden felt that as the sole MLA at that point from outside the two main parties, that she was well treated and regarded.

A view was also expressed that there were times when the two main parties got on better in private than they did in public. This, it would seem, may have been counter-productive. Both the main parties have had difficulty in bringing their party supporters with them at difficult times. Our society can only make progress if there is genuine reconciliation. For that to happen, there has to be the "brave leadership" that Claire Sugden called for. It requires for the parties to be clear that they are against sectarianism and support social integration, including in schools and housing. We seem to be a long way from achieving that. It also requires the main parties to be unapologetic to their supporters about their commitment to work in partnership and to heal divisions.

Isolation within separate communities is not assisting reconciliation: it is also financially unsustainable. How long will the UK government – and taxpayers (particularly in England) - be willing to finance such a large subvention to Northern Ireland? Much of that subvention is the cost of the social division and service duplication that continues to mark Northern Ireland.

Ironically, while the choice between UK or United Ireland represents the division between the DUP (and TUV and UUP) with Sinn Féin (and the SDLP), the symptoms of that division must be addressed irrespective of whether the north becomes part of an all-island Ireland, or continues to be Northern Ireland. For unionists, the costs of division must be addressed if the UK is to continue to be willing to pick up the bill. For republicans, they must demonstrate their capacity to be effective (and more effective than in the past) in government if they are to be in government in the south and to influence the debate around the reunification of Ireland.

One point made by several interviewees is that Sinn Féin cannot in the north be the successful advocates of a united Ireland. History prevents them winning over many of the people that need to be won over. As Peter Robinson hinted in a Queen's University lecture, the future requires a more reasoned debate over the future of Ireland than was achieved over Brexit. A compromise that keeps everyone happy with relation to the future of Northern Ireland is impossible. But to achieve the 'settled' outcome that will lead to an effective all-island state must require a significant number of Protestants, former unionists, to believe it is the best solution. Those people need to be won over by evidence.

The recently deceased former deputy First Minister of Northern Ireland, Seamus Mallon, cast doubt on the framework of the Good Friday agreement in terms of a simple majority achieving unity. "I have come increasingly to the view that the Belfast Agreement metric of a bare 50% +1 majority for unity in a Border poll will not give us the kind of agreed and peaceful Ireland we seek," he wrote.[217]

In this he is undoubtedly correct. But it does need to be stressed that this would be a fundamental change to the agreement that Mallon himself negotiated. And, as Professor Colin Harvey and others have argued, it would create a situation where a nationalist vote was worth less than a unionist vote. This is surely unacceptable and a breach of civil right principles. The answer has to be for pro-unity advocates to seek a decisive, large, majority. However, a one vote majority would, ultimately, have to be accepted.

A NEW IRELAND?

There was widespread agreement amongst those we interviewed that it would be unacceptable to expect Northern Ireland to join the Republic of Ireland as it stands. While its new social liberalism is widely welcomed across the north, its heavily criticised health system is unpopular in Northern Ireland. The housing crisis in the south is another negative. And while regional policy in the Republic is arguably better than that in the north, it is not effective enough.

"I think it is particular valuable that [an earlier] report [from the author] points out that future arrangements in any new all island Irish State should draw from best practice in either jurisdiction, such as health in the North and economics and education in the Republic," commented Former Ambassador for Ireland, Ray Bassett. "The NHS is needed in a united Ireland," said Claire Sugden. "We must have an NHS, free at the point of delivery," echoed Stephen Farry.

Andy Pollak suggested: "The idea of an all-island health service is worth considering seriously. I believe this would be a practical and mutually beneficial 'pilot' project to see how wider all-island governance could work in the longer term."

As one leading political commentator (privately) put it: "If you just called a referendum it would be lost because no one knows at present what they're voting for: a unitary state, a federal state, a confederal state, the continuation of Stormont subordinate to the Dáil? What would the currency be? What would happen to health care? Would I have to pay €100 to go to A & E? What would the question(s) be in the referendum?"

One of the contentious issues regarding unity is the speed with which it can be achieved and deciding what needs to happen prior to it being achieved. SDLP leader Colum Eastwood has said: "Those of us who believe in a New Ireland need to offer a credible and positive vision – we will not protest our way into one."[218]

Fianna Fáil's General Election manifesto of 2020 stated: "Fianna Fáil believes that unity within a shared state would be to the social, economic and cultural benefit of all the people of Ireland. The achievement of this fundamental goal through peaceful means and founded on reconciliation remains a core goal for our party." It added that the party's objectives include "deeper and wider shared public services across north and south" and promised if in government to "establish new formal structures for dialogue between the Irish and British governments, along the style of the Nordic Council of Ministers".[219][220]

THE ROLE OF THE IRISH GOVERNMENT

It is essential that there is a good relationship between the Irish state and the people and institutions of Northern Ireland. That applies irrespective of the constitutional situation of Northern Ireland. Brexit has created unhelpful, negatives stresses to those relationships. Former Taoiseach Leo Varadkar made efforts to improve relationships with civic society in the north. But as Jane Morrice observed: "We need to improve the outreach from the south to unionists and Protestants in the north. This needs to be taken seriously – very seriously. Tokenism is not enough." The election of the unionist Ian Marshall to the Senate is excellent and indicative of much more that needs to be done.

However, Varadkar reacted negatively – as did then opposition leader Micheál Martin – to the call by a thousand letter writers to establish a Citizens' Assembly to prepare for Irish unity. Despite this, academic reviews that consider the prospects and preconditions for Irish unity and also the promise by Varadkar that the Irish state would invest in Northern Irish infrastructure and university expansion does suggest that the Irish government is on the early stages of preparations for Irish unity – as a contingency consideration, if nothing else.

It is perhaps surprising that the Republic's general election of 2020 did not give any great consideration to Irish unity, despite the prominence of Sinn Féin. Little was said about SláinteCare, which many would regard as a precondition of unity and the two main parties – FG and FF – achieve a consensus in saying effectively yes to unity, but please not yet.

It would be helpful if many more people – the unionist population – looked to the Taoiseach as an advocate for their interests. As Máirtín Ó Muilleoir expressed it, "We need more 'Irish unionists' - unionists who see themselves as Irish." In truth, many unionists – as Claire Sugden elegantly explained – are comfortable as being both unionist and Irish, including by supporting the Irish rugby and cricket teams.

But for this progress to happen, change is needed in the south, to embrace not merely all the people of the north, but also to acknowledge the history of people of the north and the positive role of Protestants. "The rest of Ireland does not understand about the role of Presbyterianism, for example its role in creating the United States," explained Philip Gilliland, who is an historian as well as a lawyer. "This needs to be an all-Ireland conversation. Catholic Ireland needs to be proud of the Ulster Scots' contribution and welcome them into the family. That would be an historic meeting of minds. How do we get more people in Ireland educated about the Presbyterian role? Paisley was correct: two tribes have to get on. This is a ten year conversation. Protestant Ulster needs to go to Dublin to talk."

This progress must go beyond government. It should be noted, though, the warm praise from former Bishop Ken Good for the generosity from the Department of Foreign Affairs in supporting the Church of Ireland. Jane Morrice made the profound observation that other Irish institutions must begin to see themselves as relevant to the whole of Ireland, including the north, if the people of Northern Ireland are to see the Republic as relevant to them. "The institutions in the Republic need to reflect more of the northern culture, for example, RTE," she argued, persuasively. "RTE does not have much presence in the north and its broadcasts are not easily accessible in Northern Ireland. This restricts the level of knowledge and understanding in the north of the Republic's state and government."

This book argues that Northern Ireland is better-off as part of a reunified Ireland. But this is not a short-term project. While one recent opinion poll[221] showed significant support for a united Ireland, this is not a consistent result of all polls. And there remains much uncertainty around what people would be voting for. There needs to be an informed, open, debate on the merits of UK or UI. That debate should begin now. However, an immediate border poll might be to the benefit of those unionists who are strongly opposed to reunification and would like an early referendum that they are more likely to win and which might put the issue into a closed cupboard for several years.

It is instructive that most opinion leaders spoken with said that they did not have a clear picture of what a united Ireland would look like. Mark Durkan had both a vision and a route map towards achieving it. His plan includes clarity that Northern Ireland would become part of the existing Republic of Ireland. He believes that calling for a new constitution would create too much uncertainty and would be unacceptable to voters in the south. He also suggests that there must be bold measures to protect British identities. These include the right to continue to hold a British nationality and identity after reunification. Presumably that right could be passed down the generations.

Part of the useful ongoing debate would focus on whether the Republic should become federated, with the continuation of Stormont – and whether Stormont should be for the existing six counties, or the nine counties of Ulster. If the latter, should there also be assemblies for the other provinces? Would Stormont, and other possible assemblies, have its existing or lesser powers?

There are also issues around community identities that this section of the report has attempted to steer away from. These include flags, emblems, parades, relationships with the British Crown, the role of the

President, languages. If these could be discussed as part of an early theoretical debate, rather than later on as part of a real decision-making process, the level of contention and tension might be reduced.

It might be time, now, to move away from the terms 'unionist' and 'unionism'. It is noticeable that Arlene Foster has used the term 'Ulster British', as has the New Decade New Approach document. That is more durable and sustainable term, which applies whatever the constitutional future of Northern Ireland.

Perhaps the first priority, though, if the Republic is genuinely committed to eventual reunification is the reform of its health service. The cost of reform would be substantial in moving to a free at point of delivery model, but discussions around this change could begin soon. Failure to achieve this would be regarded by many in the north as an impediment to reunification.

As the main parties ally themselves closely with Christian values, it might be appropriate to quote former Bishop Ken Good's comments. "Generosity needs to be shown. As Christians, we need to be proactive with forgiveness. This has been overlooked. Christianity has forgiveness at its heart."

Perhaps the most telling remark made by an interviewee was by DUP MLA Mervyn Storey. Talking in general about Northern Irish society, he said: "There will be change." He added: "I am against a single Irish jurisdiction – but I would have to accept it if there was a vote and that was the outcome. Unionists must not think that day could not come. There has to be an honest discussion around the benefits or disadvantages of being in the UK or a united Ireland. The [author's] reports, along with others, can inform a discussion. There is a lesson from what is happening in the Republic for everyone, including in unionism."

12 CONVERSATION PIECES

“

MARK DALY,
Irish senator

“There is a need for action now: policy neglect seldom goes unpunished. The future is a united Ireland as provided for under the Good Friday Agreement, with protection for the culture and identity of unionists and within the European Union. The Good Friday Agreement is, in effect, the pathway to the peaceful and prosperous unity of Ireland and her people.”

“

DENIS BRADLEY,
Co-chair, Consultative Group on the Past

“Our problem at the moment is we don’t know where we’re going. Well, we don’t know where we’re going at the moment, we may have very strong ideas of where we may go in the future and where we should go in the future. Just in this moment in time, it’s not very clear.

“The real question for us is, can we move beyond that [Brexit-related] unsettlement in England? To actually engage at a real and honest and radical engagement in this island.... What we need is an all-island forum.

What we need is conversations to start. What we need is engagement from all the different parts of this island... I do see unionism's propensity to go back in on itself and at difficult moments not to engage - I can understand why this is. They come from a position that nationalism can lose 20 times or 40 times. Unionism can only lose once. They will become incredibly defensive."

“

MIKE NESBITT MLA,

Former leader, Ulster Unionist Party

"What concerns me from a unionist perspective is that we are in danger of becoming the famous frog that Charles Handy used to talk about. He was a business guru who said if you take a frog and put it in a pan of cold water and very, very slowly heat it to boiling point, the frog dies because at no point does it realise the environment around it has changed until the point it's too late. Unionism needs to look and recognise that the environment around us is changing. The demographics are changing. That does not mean a united Ireland is inevitable, but it is something we need to be aware of. Scottish nationalism is a threat to the union, English nationalism is a threat to the union and I would go as far as to say that I believe the DUP and some of their policies, attitudes and tone is a long term threat to the union. So I would like to see civic unionism becoming more active."

“

MERVYN STOREY MLA,

Former DUP finance minister

"I want a peaceful, settled, prosperous Northern Ireland. We are not living in the 1960s. There will be change. We need to be future focused. While I'd like past crimes to be dealt with through the courts, there is little chance sadly in many cases of getting justice for most past crimes. We've had a conflict management process, rather than a reconciliation process. There is the challenge.

"There was too much focus on the relationship between Ian Paisley and Martin McGuinness. We (in the DUP) don't know who is in charge of Sinn Féin. Too many unionists do not understand the dynamics and difficulties within republicanism. Too many unionist voters do not understand the differences between dissidents and Sinn Féin.

The society I would like is: respect for the rule of law; fairness, for example in employment. There should be responsibility and accountability in government. I want devolution to work. A caring society that supports people in crisis. To move beyond the platitudes of respect. I am anti-abortion and pro-traditional marriage, but I must recognise that others in my community have different views from me in this. Government in future should be outcomes focused.

"I am against a single Irish jurisdiction – but I would have to accept it if there was a vote and that was the outcome. Unionists must not think that day could not come. There has to be an honest discussion around the benefits or disadvantages of being in the UK or a united Ireland. The reports [by this author], along with others, can inform a discussion. There is a lesson from what is happening in the Republic for everyone, including in unionism."

"

JOHN KYLE,

Belfast city councillor, former leader, Progressive Unionist Party

"If you want to create something different you've got to create the environment, the circumstances, the conditions in which something different can emerge. At the moment we are stuck in ruts and so we need to shake things up, create some new opportunities for people to debate, to meet, to argue, to make decisions, to plan, to take initiatives. We are going to have to create those opportunities, otherwise if politicians' position of power is not under threat they are happy to just let things continue to trundle on."

“

LINDA ERVINE,

Irish language teacher

"We've got to reach across the divide. Sadly 20 years after the Good Friday Agreement we are still very much a divided community, which frustrates me greatly. There's been a change in narrative. We have become less sectarian where it's about religion and become more sectarian where it's become about politics. The game now is to vilify people because of their politics.

"Unfortunately that's played out by our politicians because it sadly works well to polarise people. So it is to educate young people to realise that because somebody disagrees with you, it doesn't make them the devil. They have an entitlement to a different point of view. We can still build a Northern Ireland that works. People have to stop being defensive, stop looking for offence. We have to have graciousness, generosity and recognise there are certain differences.

"I feel things are changing and not just in Northern Ireland. Things are changing in the UK. We've seen movement in Scotland where there was a referendum which didn't end up in an independent Scotland, but that is a change that has a possibility and might come. If I could personally wave my magic wand, I would like to see a federation of islands. The identity issue with an all Ireland isn't an issue for me. The issue for me would be the practical outcomes, the National Health [Service]. I like the National Health [Service], I like being British, I like enjoying the British way of life. For me, if a constitutional change has to come, I want to keep very close links with the rest of the UK and I wonder is there some way that a new discussion could be opened up.

"I have been surprised at some of the people from the unionist community who have started to say, 'Well actually, I would be in favour of going into Ireland'. So there is a change in mindset and the only way we can respectfully deal with that and acknowledge that is by giving people space to talk without attacking them."

“

CLAIRE SUGDEN MLA,

Independent unionist and former justice minister

“The values I want in society are respect, the appreciation that everyone is different and for that difference to be embraced. Difference can be contentious. I want empathy and compromise. You can’t get agreement if you don’t have empathy. It needs to be understood that we are the products of our experiences and of our families. I understand why people did things, even if I don’t agree with what they did. I do have a specific designation as a unionist and I think that is right. We need to de-sensitise the concepts of unionism and nationalism.

“Justice is about upholding the rule of law. Often what people mean by justice is fairness. Truth is also difficult, because it means different things for different people. Social justice is another important concept. The different narratives should be told.

“My unionism is practical. I believe the best place for Northern Ireland for now is part of the UK. I am not convinced that even after Brexit that the best place for Northern Ireland will be outside the UK. If there were circumstances in which on a practical basis we would be better off in a united Ireland then I would consider that. Unionism is also part of my culture. Northern Ireland is my home and I wouldn’t leave. I’m happy to say that I’m Irish, Northern Irish and British. The Good Friday Agreement allows us to say that we are both Irish and British. The Good Friday Agreement is not the end game for those pursuing nationalism. In 1998, unionism thought that it was the compromise of both ideologies; nationalism saw it as a stepping stone. I am interested in the ideas of a ‘new Ireland’; I’m not sure how those proposing it will find a purpose for unionism after unification....

“The NHS is needed in a united Ireland. Sinn Féin needs to go on a journey. What I like about the Republic is that it is structured around issues, like the Department for Children. It is very focused on outcomes. And I like the voluntary coalition structure in the south. The Republic is being brave, for example on abortion and same sex marriage. It is helping Ireland move forward. I crave leadership in Northern Ireland.”

"

NAOMI LONG MLA,

Justice minister, leader Alliance Party, former MEP & MP

"What has happened over time is that the politics has become more and more precious about its own position. So what we have had are parties that are more focused on their leadership role and less on the engagement side.... But I also think there's been constriction in the political system too where we've gone from a situation where we had an inclusive process to one which very rapidly became a kind of four party process as it was and we had to battle for it to be even a five party process - to what then emerged more recently, which wasn't even a two party process, in that the governments weren't even involved in that two party process. It was literally just the DUP and Sinn Féin.

"And it doesn't work because if people are locked into very fixed positions and they just repeatedly meet with each other to discuss those positions, there's no new thinking, there's no creativity, but there's also no opportunity to bring new issues or ideas to the table that could allow people to start to move their position.... I think that some of that civic society conversation can be had at a different level where it's not a political threat to anyone, but it's actually exploring relationships."

"

PETER SHERIDAN,

Chief executive, Co-operation Ireland

"The core values for transition out of violence are: peace keeping; peace-making, peace building (which is where we are now) and peace sharing (which we have not yet reached).

"We have got through the peace-making phase. We reached an agreement on how we are governed. But we have not agreed about how we learn to live together. We remain in a cold war situation. We had 18 peace walls before the Good Friday Agreement, we have 88 now. The institutions of the Good Friday Agreement were only ever supposed to be stepping stones to the next stage. Sectarianism is still there. Politicians are not genuinely committed to the Good Friday Agreement.

"People should ask the political parties what they are going to do. Ask unionists what they will do for nationalist and republicans. Ask republicans what will do to protect PUL communities. Good rights are what you will do to protect others. We have never got to the stage where we can walk in other people's shoes. But the good news is that everything is shift-able.

"We have to deal with the past. We need to debate the past and deal with it. Universities are a good place for debates. We will never do justice on the scale of the injustice. There should have been a Department for Reconciliation within the Executive. We should have had a future facing government. We don't do enough to tell unionists that we will protect unionist identity. We need to convince a generation of young people."

In a subsequent interview, he added: "One of the weaknesses of the Good Friday Agreement was that we managed to get all of the political parties in Northern Ireland to concede to the British government of Tony Blair. We managed to get them all to concede to the Irish government of Bertie Ahern. We managed to get them all to concede to the American government, of Bill Clinton. But they didn't concede to each other."

"

BRIAN FEENEY,

Political commentator

"Taken with the simultaneous British-Irish Agreement which replaced the 1985 Anglo-Irish Agreement, the Good Friday Agreement is in effect the constitution of Northern Ireland. With the repeal of the 1920 Government of Ireland Act in 1998 which had repeated the British parliament's overall jurisdiction, the GFA defined the relations between Ireland north and south and between Britain and Ireland east-west, and instead of the overall jurisdiction of Westminster for the future status of the region, vested that in a majority of the people of the north. The phrase, 'the people of Northern Ireland' is defined in the British-Irish Agreement Annex 2 for the purpose of giving effect to this provision to elucidate par. (vi) of Article 1 of the GFA.

"As an international treaty the GFA, and therefore the north's constitution, cannot be altered without the consent of both the British and Irish governments whereas previously it had been in the power of Westminster alone. There are few places anywhere else in the world (Alto Adige/ Sud Tyrol is one) where one part of a state is subject to an agreed arrangement for an input from another state about the present and future status that part of the state. As a result, the north is constitutionally a semi-detached part of the UK, with or without a trade barrier in the Irish Sea."

"

PETER OSBORNE,

Former chair of the Parades Commission and of the Community Relations Council

"I am a fan of things like Citizens' Assemblies that we've seen working in the Republic of Ireland very, very successfully. I was down at the Citizens' Assembly that dealt with the environment: what I saw there was a hundred people drawn from civil society, randomly sampled, geographically spread, different genders, different age ranges, different socio-economic backgrounds, no political baggage. They were intensely exploring issues from the perspective of the evidence, not from the perspective of anything around political politics, or what constituency they would have to represent, or who might have more influence on who gives them votes. They explored the evidence and they came up with conclusions that were just logical that therefore would be good policy based on good evidence.

"When you look at some of the big successes of the peace process over the last 20 years, two of the big successes, I would argue, are policing and parading. What do they have in common? When policing reform was mooted and then processed, you had a panel from civil society led by

Chris Patten, with people from Northern Ireland who came up with that report and shaped policing and the change in policing."

"

ALAN McBRIDE,

Victims campaigner

"Politics here isn't working.... The whole Brexit debate has poisoned the attitudes of the political parties here and also in relation between north and south and east and west. So we've gone backwards in the last couple of years. But I hope that doesn't mean that it has to always be like that. We can go forward better in the future.

"I believe that the only thing that's keeping us apart at the minute, certainly politically, is to do with attitude. To be honest with you, the DUP do not want parity of esteem with republicans. They want to live in a very British Northern Ireland, flying the Union flag, where there's no real rights for Irish language speakers. On the other side of the coin, Sinn Féin appear to be on this anti-British, anti-unionist, anti-loyalist journey: if you talk to grassroots loyalists they'll say that they're trying to strip every vicissitude of Britishness away from local government and from the public spaces. To what extent that's true, I don't know.

"But I do think those attitudes need to be reconciled in some way. I talk about the notion of what it means to be a good neighbour.... But when people vote in the way that they do, they are not voting for government, they're not voting for a Northern Ireland that's going to work, they are actually voting for those political parties to hold the line. And those parties are holding the line. You couldn't fault them for that. [But] they're not only failing their own people, they're failing everybody in this society.

“

JIM DORNAN,
Professor of health

“I am welcoming civic nationalism, I’m welcoming civic unionism, but I’m even more welcoming a combination of both. And there’s a great opportunity for the middle ground which is becoming a very interesting part of politics to look at, to come together and advise the wings on either side as we have in this part of the world and try to de-sectarianise politics in Northern Ireland once and for all. We look at every tenet of our society, everything – culture, health, education, agriculture, fisheries, digital age - everything. We need to look at the experts in our society and bring them together.

“Are we as a people happy to continue to have a subvention for the next 50 years? Does that make us proud? Is that good? Is that the best way to use our resources? I very much would like to see the Secretary of State set-up or support a Civic Forum and also support a movement that would actually produce an independent dossier, but I would like to see her coming in behind it and see everybody, all the political parties saying, ‘Yes, let’s have facts as we move forward’ to when we eventually do get to the situation where we can address what dispensation is best for this island.

“Ireland is a Goldilocks-sized country for health provision. We can cherry pick the best of health provision throughout the world and introduce it to Ireland. The health service is a wonderful concept. Prevention is important and treatments are important. Big decisions have to be made. Our society has to take more responsibility for its health. We can’t just keep abusing everything and expect an NHS to collect us at the end of the day. So somewhere between Norway and New Zealand would be my perfect health service. In New Zealand, they have a no-blame culture, so you don’t have to prove that somebody’s done something wrong to get help to look after your child if it’s got a genetic or an acquired problem.”

"

CONAL McFEELY,

Community activist

"As a society still emerging from conflict we must collectively not allow ourselves to make the same political mistakes and the failure of governance that we've done in the past, but sadly I believe that we are at the moment.

"The Good Friday Agreement, to all intents and purposes, [was about] social transformation. I view social transformation as something that looks at the economic, cultural, educational, environmental needs of society. The focus went on the main political parties and it didn't look at society. All the structures we had in place were quite narrow. We need to have policies that address where people are - and lots of people in this society are denied the opportunity to go into the world of work. A lot of people are being denied further education opportunities.

"The economic agenda rolled-out over the last 20 odd years is quite narrow. It is predicated on one economic model. It needs to be much broader. It needs to embrace the social economy as part of creating a mixed and balanced economy. People have been looking after the few, instead of looking after the many. The private sector will do certain things. But if you look at where people feel left behind, it's those communities that have suffered most as a result of the conflict. It tends to be in working class Protestant and working class Catholic areas where the conflict was fought out. That's where the highest levels of poverty exist and the highest levels of economic inactivity. Our political elite have been following an economic agenda that's not addressing that."

"

ANTHONY RUSSELL,

Historian

"Civil society has been moving. In the past when the unionist peered over the border into the south they saw exactly what they predicted a hundred years ago and they predicted a priest ridden Free State and that came to pass under de Valera when it became a Republic. But southern society has changed enormously. It has become much more liberal, the power of the Catholic Church has weakened. Particularly from a unionist merchant point of view, the fact that the Celtic Tiger roared and then aborted, it fell back a bit but recovered to a large extent. I think unionists admire that. So I would be hopeful that unionists looking over the border are now more attracted towards the society in the south, even though it is probably now too liberal for them."

"

ANDY POLLAK,

Founding director of the Centre for Cross Border Studies

"I like (former Attorney General) John Rogers' suggestion that the Irish Constitution should be amended to recognise 'the plural origins of our people'. People in the South are going to have to get used to the idea that in the event of unity constitution, flag and anthem (in order to incorporate 'Britishness' into Irish symbols) will all have to change. It won't be easy to persuade them.

"I also like (Senior Counsel) Des Murphy's idea of an independent international mediator (or maybe an international Opsahl-style commission) that could draw up proposals for the future governance of Ireland (within the framework of the Good Friday Agreement) - to be put to people north and south in a referendum. I would regard this as much more sensible than a crude border poll, which, in the event of a 50%+1 vote for unity, would lead to renewed mayhem.

"The idea of an all-island health service is also worth considering seriously. I believe this would be a practical and mutually beneficial 'pilot' project to see how wider all-island governance could work in the longer term.

"On the wider issue I think it needs to be spelled just what an extraordinarily liberal society the Republic has become in a short time.

It is now one of the most liberal countries in Europe: liberal abortion and same sex marriage overwhelmingly passed by referenda; gay, half-Indian Taoiseach; over 17% of the population foreign-born and not a whiff of a right-wing reaction."

JANE MORRICE,

Former Women's Coalition MLA and
Deputy speaker of Northern Ireland Assembly,
Former head of the European Commission's Office in Belfast,
Former Northern Ireland deputy equality commissioner,
Initiator of petition for Northern Ireland to remain part of the EU.

"The values I want in society are honesty, integrity, equality, human rights, inclusion, mutual respect, understanding, tolerance, justice. Those values are European-wide and not linked to being north or south of the border.

"Reconciliation across the island is essential. I was present at the all-island forum on Brexit in Dundalk, which Barnier attended, but unionists were poorly represented. Outreach from the south to unionists and Protestants in the north should perhaps be more creative. This needs to be taken seriously – very seriously. Tokenism is not enough. Ian Marshall joining the Senate is good, but we have been here before with northern unionists sitting in the Senate.

"The institutions in the Republic need to reflect more of the northern culture, for example, RTE. RTE does not have much presence in the north and its broadcasts are not easily accessible in Northern Ireland. This restricts the level of knowledge and understanding in the north of the Republic's state and government."

"

STEPHEN FARRY MP,

Deputy leader of the Alliance Party,
Former Northern Ireland employment minister

"I have a liberal perspective, which is a flexible term. I believe in rights, equality, fairness, a rights-based approach, empowerment, democracy, the rule of law.... Northern Ireland is still marked by sectarian division. This leads to different people having different life chances and can determine where they can live.

"The Good Friday Agreement was about creating new relationships across the islands, but it was imperfect. It was a means towards a reconciled and peaceful society. There were unresolved issues at the time - decommissioning was too slow, legacy, the rule of law - and these caused difficulties. That led to greater support for parties that took a hard line. There was no shared vision. Support for progress was always limited and qualified. In particular this was because the parties had different constitutional objectives.

"The Executive became a transactional clearing house. Lots of policy was determined outside the Executive. Proposals for health service reform were not discussed inside the Executive. Meetings were often unpleasant. There was little conversation about how do we deal with the big issues. The 'zero sum game' led to cronyism and lack of accountability, which in part contributed to the collapse.

"There was a conscious effort to keep constitutional issues out of the Executive, such as legacy, flags. These issues were discussed in other places. There was never a conversation at the Executive about segregation. It was about doing business as quickly as possible and get out. Meetings might be delayed by two, three or four hours and then the meeting last just ten minutes. One meeting that was scheduled for 2.30 actually began at 7.30. The Budget for 2016/17 for £11bn was tabled 30 minutes before the meeting and agreed on the nod.

"Sinn Féin were not very good at government. Lots of things had to be run through the wider party.... There was a lack of generosity by DUP to Sinn Féin and to other parties, especially after 2012....

"On the question of reunification, I am open minded. I don't have a fixed mind regarding UK or united Ireland. We must have reconciliation, a liberal society. The Alliance contains some members who are unionists and others who are nationalist.

"Against: subvention is a powerful economic argument. We must have an NHS, free at the point of delivery. Pro: Brexit, especially a hard Brexit; a united Ireland provides a route back into the EU; social policy, RoI is rapidly changing and more attractive than NI. I am reconsidering my position.

"Any discussion risks polarising society. So we don't want to jump in. The present priority is delivery via a Northern Ireland Executive. The tipping point would be a hard Brexit and bad economic outcomes would be influential. Northern Ireland is not yet ready for this discussion. Nothing is guaranteed on the future of the subvention, or whether there will be change to the Barnett Formula.

"I have not really thought about what the future would be in a united Ireland. There needs to be respect for British and Irish identities. Not simply assimilation. There needs to be change on both sides.

"If it happened, a lot of people in Northern Ireland would be very unhappy. It might involve a constitutional settlement with unionist representatives and protection of the unionist population and their rights. There might be a consociational structure in UI, as in Belgium, where things are done in accordance with a convention. Northern Ireland does it constitutionally."

"

MÁIRTÍN Ó MUILLEOIR,

Former Sinn Féin finance minister

"We need to adopt the values appropriate for a wounded society. The priorities should be: build the peace, foster reconciliation. There are lots of divided societies in Europe. But while there are divisions, those are different. No one has a clear answer on how to achieve this. Justice: you can't have reconciliation without justice. Which also means civil rights.

You have to look forward, not live in the past. The Stormont House Agreement found a way to deal with justice, while moving forward. There's a balance.

"The aspirations for a united Ireland should be: prosperity; a shared future, which includes prosperity for all; no dysfunction, no peace walls, people should be safe to walk where they want; the normalising of peace; a modern European society. We should be international leaders. Ireland should be global in outlook.

"How to move ahead? We need more 'Irish unionists' - unionists who see themselves as Irish. No one has set out the form a united Ireland would take. I don't believe it would be like East Germany joining West Germany, it would be more complex.

"The future depends on the people who are proud of being Irish while being unionists, not those who despise the Irish language and are difficult to deal with. Irish unionism is a good tradition.

"My learnings as mayor of Belfast were that if you meet unionists half way, they will meet you; unionists are ahead of their political leadership; there is a real desire for change I found people more welcoming than might be expected.

"It is possible to do deals without trust. There has to be a trade-off. Reaching out to unionism is an urgent task. We are not doing enough to build that bridge. There are big challenges for Sinn Féin.

"No one has really imagined the future, for example how the Dáil would work, for example unionists in government. I would find it easier to imagine unionists in a continuing Stormont Assembly. The Good Friday Agreement was only a staging post. I have never thought about the role of the DUP and UUP in the Dáil."

MARK DURKAN,

Former deputy first minister and
Former SDLP MP, leader and finance minister

"The Good Friday Agreement provides for two choices on the

constitutional status of Northern Ireland - United Kingdom or a united Ireland. Unionist and nationalist aspirations are equally legitimate, therefore the threshold for majority consent in a referendum for either option must be equal. True parity of esteem cannot require a larger majority for one consent-based option rather than the other.

"Neither unionists nor nationalists would be working for just a 50% plus one outcome. Each would hope for bigger margins! But in the event of a narrow margin either way, the result has to be respected.

"The SDLP set out in papers [in 2003 and 2005] that the Good Friday Agreement must be seen to endure beyond any referendum result. In the event of a vote to change the north's constitutional status, the principles, promises and precepts of the Agreement should still hold as mandated in 1998. The Agreement provides for 'review' arrangements. Such review mechanisms would be the channels for adjustments to be made in institutional structures to be compatible with change in constitutional status and to remain compatible with the Agreement.

"We set this out to allay any apprehension that having a referendum or its possible outcome would forfeit the unique standing of the Agreement. We also did it to show that it was not just unionists who were challenged by the Agreement to recondition their assumptions. This was a way of showing that nationalists had to look at a united Ireland under the light of the Agreement. This means allowing for a continuing Strand One and embedding Strand Three's East-West structures for the future (using reviews to enhance these).

"There could not be a purely internal settlement in the north or inside the UK. But we can also accept that, even in a united Ireland, there would not be a purely internal settlement on this island. To take account of unionists' identity and ongoing affinity we have to think about more than just British passports for those who want them. As we have sought a direct northern voice in a reformed Seanad, then the "do unto others..." rule should apply in a united Ireland. This would not mean all institutions staying static in a united Ireland as a new dynamic would be created by the scale of northern representation in an all-Ireland parliament as compared with Westminster. That would include a substantive unionist presence.

"Recalibrating the devolution envelope and re-gearing for all-island administration and legislation can be achieved by agreement using the modalities of the Agreement, building confidence and furthering reconciliation on the island and between these islands.

"This sort of understanding avoids the false precondition of having to secure unionist agreement to a united Ireland before a referendum. It also avoids the false promise of having a referendum which, if passed, only invites negotiations which could be frustrated. The Brexit negotiation debacle is a warning that those who value the unity by consent precept of the Agreement need to have a sat-nav for how a positive result is advanced consistent with the Agreement."

"

PHILIP GILLILAND,

Lawyer and Anglican

"We've been given a gift in this process which is called Brexit, because it's allowed those of us who are from a Protestant background, which is me, to be able to talk about the heresy of the united Ireland in a way that is not heresy. It's allowed us to talk about the possibility of constitutional change in a way that doesn't seem to be disloyal to the tribe, because clearly for many of us, Brexit is nuts.

"That sounds very disrespectful to people. I should really retract that. People are entitled to their view, if they think it's the right thing to do, brilliant. Fill your boots. That's grand, but it clearly has changed the dynamic between how we deal with our neighbours in the south and how we deal with our neighbours in Britain. It's shone a light on the fact that the British don't really know or care very much about Northern Ireland. We knew that anyway."

In an earlier interview Philip explained: "My values are those of the Taoiseach: socially liberal; fiscally, moderately conservative. I believe people should live according to the values they espouse, without hypocrisy and with tolerance. I believe in inclusion, including all indigenous and non-indigenous communities. In Northern Ireland, that explicitly means educating children together - otherwise people will never escape their 'mono-ness'.

"Sinn Féin does not articulate what it means by 'equality'. It can mean nothing more than our tribe must have the same as the other tribe. Equality can mean meritocracy, equality of opportunity - which is what we must strive towards. What does justice mean? We need truth and honesty about the past. Administratively, justice in respect of Troubles-related crimes is not possible. The forgotten people are the victims. What we need is truth. We need that from government and from republicans and from loyalists.

"We are in a system of voluntary segregation. Better government would help to deal with this and could lead to a process of desegregation. But who can govern us to lead us into desegregation? The only solution that we have not tried is for the Republic to do this.

"The UK government is not interested in direct rule and has no appetite for this. We need to explore another approach that could work and that is a united Ireland. Brexit has changed everything. It has helped Protestants to talk about a united Ireland in ways they never have before. Protestant business leaders are now talking about Brexit changing things. The east around Belfast is much more of a British economy, but the west is much less.

"As a Protestant it makes me wonder what it was about a united Ireland that we are supposed to be afraid of. For unionists a hundred years ago my guess is that their views were informed by three things:

1 Why leave the world's largest trading bloc,

2 Home rule would be Rome rule,

3 Bigotry.

"The theocracy is now in Northern Ireland, not the Republic of Ireland, which is a socially liberal country. Numbers one and two no longer apply, which only leaves number three and I don't want to be a bigot.

"The rest of Ireland does not understand about the culture and heritage of Ulster Scots Presbyterianism, for example its role in the creation of the United States. This needs to be an all-Ireland conversation. Catholic Ireland needs to be proud of the Ulster Scots' contribution and welcome them back into the family. That would be an historic meeting of minds. How do we get more people in Ireland educated about the Presbyterian role? Paisley was correct on one thing: the two tribes have to find a way to get on. This is a ten year conversation. Protestant Ulster needs to go to Dublin to talk.

"I want a unitary Ireland, not a federal Ireland. A federal Ireland would do very little for the North West/Derry, which desperately needs to see the removal of the border. I would be against the continuation of Stormont for this reason, and also because the inherent tribal stalemate means it cannot function in anything other than a populist fashion. It would be different if it was a nine counties Stormont.

"How does it happen? If it's initiated by Catholic politicians, it can't happen. It has to come from Protestant Northern Ireland and from Dublin."

13
A PROGRAMME FOR AN INTEGRATED IRELAND

THE VISION contained in the Good Friday Agreement has not been realised. Specifically, the focus of Strand Two – co-operation north-south – has been sidelined and the envisaged joint work on key cross-border programmes has been held back. The result is both a lack of economic progress and also a failure to achieve the financial and social benefits that would have been achieved by greater cross-border joint working.

It is essential that the three governments – the Northern Ireland Executive, the UK government and the Irish government – recommit to the GFA and reinvigorate it, in particular with the regards to the areas of co-operation specified in the GFA. In addition, in the context of Brexit, it is essential to create stronger east-west dialogue, which is to include the minimisation of trading barriers between Northern Ireland (and the Irish Republic) and GB.

A genuine all-island economy will bring immense benefits to the population of both jurisdictions. Wealth needs to be spread to all parts of the population. This requires a strong regional policy. A more effective regional and sub-regional economic policy will relieve cost pressures in Dublin, while improving prosperity in the West.

THE CREATION OF A STRONGER ALL-ISLAND ECONOMY WOULD INVOLVE:

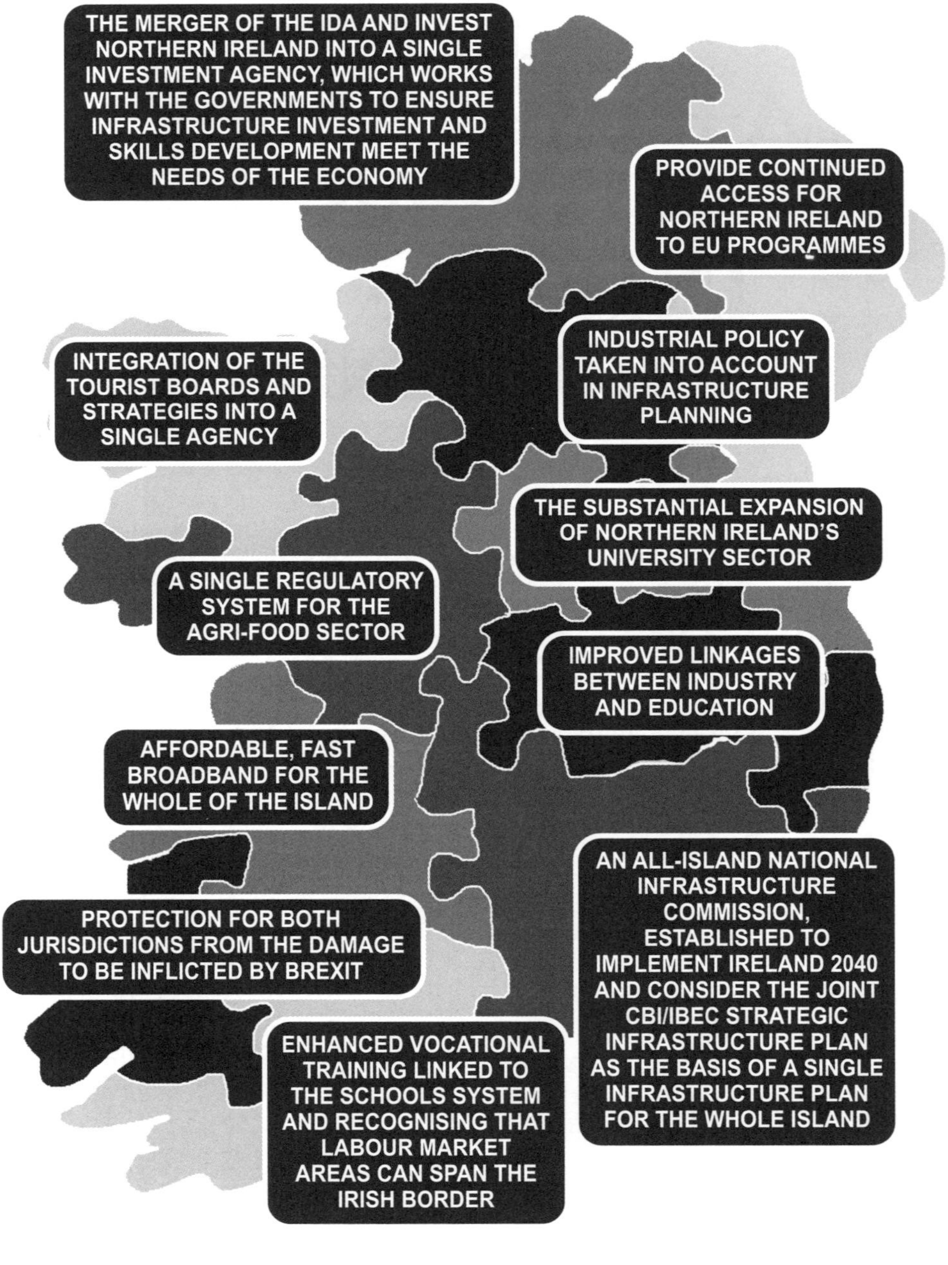

Northern Ireland should be designated a Special Economic Zone in recognition of its particular economic challenges, through the lack of an effective sub-regional policy and the particular and damaging impact of Brexit.

INFRASTRUCTURE

An all-island Ireland Infrastructure Commission should be established to implement Ireland 2040 and consider the joint CBI/IBEC strategic infrastructure plan as the basis of a single infrastructure plan for the whole island. Reform is required of infrastructure planning, on both sides of the border.

Both the Republic and Northern Ireland have encountered serious problems with major capital programmes. An integrated single body should oversee and control major infrastructure and other capital schemes on both sides of the border, bringing together the best Irish expertise to ensure that the two jurisdictions have integrated infrastructure, with improvements delivered on a value for money basis, on budget and on time.

The Ireland Infrastructure Commission's role must include planning for an all-island enhanced public transport system, to reduce car dependency, reduce carbon emissions and support cross-border economic integration and co-operation, including for health services. New ticketing systems, including online and cross-border arrangements, would make public transport more attractive and easier to navigate.

More investment is required in electric vehicle charging infrastructure, to boost the electric vehicle market and reduce carbon emissions from transport. This needs to be backed by tax incentives to purchase clean vehicles and to create disincentives to use diesel and petrol engine vehicles. Planning regulations need to be harmonised on a cross-border basis and updated to facilitate electric vehicle charging at apartment blocks and demanding low emission requirements.

Similarly, more intervention and stronger strategic direction is required to continue the clean-up of Ireland's energy distribution systems and reduce industrial and household carbon emissions. This requires more than tax incentives, though these are important and should be harmonised on an all-island basis. There needs to be a single, effectively enforced, cross-border, waste management system, that is hard on waste dumping.

An island-wide Green New Deal would create large numbers of jobs, while making an important contribution to achieving carbon reduction targets. Both jurisdictions need to increase their use of renewable sources of energy and reduce the use of fossil fuels, especially coal, peat and oil, but also including gas. Moves must include access to low cost financing, possibly including the involvement of credit unions. Social housing providers must be engaged as full partners in the move to low emission household.

Ireland needs to have a single tax system that applies on both sides of the border. At present the Republic has a corporation tax rate of 12.5% and that needs to apply on both sides of the border to ensure there is not an artificial incentive to locate in the Republic rather than the north. There should be the gradual move towards the harmonisation of other tax rates and systems, including income tax, property tax and VAT. Doing this by stages would reduce any shock from a big bang approach.

While the Republic is very effective in attracting FDI, more could be done to promote the expansion and productivity of the SME sector. New measures are required to support SMEs in growing their output, employment and productivity. The objective should be for the island of Ireland to be one of the world's foremost economies for the establishment and growth of SMEs – helping to make Ireland as strong in indigenous business development as it is in attracting FDI. For this to happen, it is necessary for higher education based R&D to transfer into the private sector and for SMEs to build productivity and learn from best practice.

Brexit may lead to a reduction in employment regulation in Great Britain. It is important that both Irish jurisdictions stick to the EU's approach of employment rights protection. This should involve the abolition of zero hours contracts, except where these are of benefit to employees. The objective is have a high waged economy, with protected employment rights. But it is important to protect the tax base from manipulation through bogus self-employment. A single enforcement regime that operates in both jurisdictions would help protect the tax base and be in a better position to tackle rogue employers that operate on both sides of the border.

It is essential that as Ireland moves towards a more integrated, all-island, economy, that it ensures that all parts of the island benefit. To achieve this it is essential that a more effective regional and sub-regional policy base is put in place. Specifically, the North West of both jurisdictions has been left behind, while the border region has challenges that must be overcome.

Several steps will help to address these weaknesses: the IDA should be expanded to absorb Invest NI; the IDA's objectives to spread investment to all areas should be applied to Northern Ireland as well as the Republic; special economic development zones should be established in Northern Ireland and the border region; and more assistance should be given to rural enterprises, including for non-profit distributing businesses that can help sustain and strengthen rural communities.

Both IDA and Invest Northern Ireland – but especially Invest Northern Ireland – have been criticised for failing to sufficiently promote sub-regional investment and job creation, focusing on areas with high unemployment and economic inactivity. They have also been criticised for not doing enough to support the economy in rural areas. The policy of Invest Northern Ireland was developed after a review conducted by the former vice-chancellor of Ulster University, Richard Barnett, which recommended there should not be a focus on sub-regional development, or localised employment targets focused on locations with higher levels of unemployment.

Businesses need finance. Ireland suffered from a catastrophic collapse in its banking sector in 2008/9. More needs to be done to develop a properly regulated, stable and independent Irish banking sector, which benefits from its position within the European Union and eurozone. SMEs and mortgage borrowers need access to affordable loans. More needs to be done to protect, sustain and benefit from Ireland's credit union sector. Vulture funds need to be fully regulated, with borrowers transferred to these offshore funds adequately protected. Consideration should be given to the creation of a state enterprise bank, to provide sources of capital – including equity – to emerging businesses in strategically important sectors that will help build Ireland's economy.

Housing is unaffordable for many people in the Republic, with housing supply inadequate in Dublin in particular. More needs to be done to increase supply. This requires a greater focus on the provision of city centre apartments – in Northern Ireland's cities, as well as in the cities of the Republic. This will provide sustainable and mixed communities. To address affordability, institutions will need to increase their investments into the sector to provide greater diversity of tenure.

The relationship between education, skills training, employment and economic development is inextricable. While the focus of education must be for personal development, it must also provide pupils and students with the skills base to improve their prospects for employment and a good income, as well as providing employers and prospective employers a skilled labour market from which to employ.

For these reasons, it is essential that Northern Ireland's education system must be substantially reformed. It is clear that there are far too few university places, leading to insufficient graduates within Northern Ireland's labour market. A greater focus is needed on apprenticeships and vocational training in both the north and the Republic. Relationships between post-primary schools and vocational training schemes need to be strengthened as a measure to reduce the level of school drop-outs and the unacceptably high number of school leavers (mostly boys) in Northern Ireland without adequate basic skills in English, maths and IT.

Employers should be offered sufficient incentives to encourage them to engage in skills training programmes, to assist with skills development. This is particularly important for SMEs, which are the most likely to benefit through improved productivity and learning from R&D. Higher education institutions in both jurisdictions need higher levels of funding, especially those in Northern Ireland. This may need to be financed by modest increases to tuition fees.

Although the Republic of Ireland is often criticised for its policies of low tax, aimed at boosting FDI, it has one of Europe's most progressive tax systems in terms of income tax. In other words, those who earn the most pay a much higher rate of tax than those who earn less. This is fair and should be the basis for the principles behind taxation going forward.

At the same time, it must be recognised that global pressures leading to reviews of corporate tax policy may lead to future reductions in the total tax take. It is therefore necessary to adopt fiscal policies that are not over-reliant on corporate tax revenues, with the state generating fiscal surpluses that buffer the government should corporate tax revenues reduce in future years. Those surpluses should also be sufficient to address the costs of unification, with a likely necessary moderate subvention needed once Northern Ireland becomes part of a unified Ireland.

However, with global interest rates at historic low levels, Ireland – either the existing Republic, or a future unified Ireland – should not be scared of borrowing. It is likely that interest rates will remain low for a number of years and it makes sense to borrow to invest, in particular in infrastructure, skills and carbon reduction. This will help build a sustainable economy, in better shape to weather future challenges.

The integration of the two jurisdictions should boost the economy of both parts of the Ireland, by expanding markets and reducing costs, for example of health and other public service provision. Some private sector markets in the Republic of Ireland are not subject to sufficient competition[222], leading to excessive costs for childcare, insurance and energy, for example. The integration of the two jurisdictions should increase market size and reduce consumer costs in both parts of the island.

For reasons of both principle and good practice, stronger state intervention is required to address market weaknesses. This should involve more support for childcare provision, making it affordable and also to provide a more integrated environment for pre-school children in Northern Ireland.

Further steps are needed to strengthen the all-island integrated energy market and to bring down the cost of energy, while further increasing the supply of renewable energy. This involves the construction of a second cross-border electricity inter-connector, helping to integrate electricity supply and strengthening the electricity grid in parts of the island that are currently poorly served. This should be backed by strengthening the powers of the energy regulators, who should move towards merger as a single all-island energy regulator.

PROTECTING AGRICULTURE AND FOOD PRODUCTION

Agriculture and agri-food represent one of the economy's most important sectors, in both the Republic and Northern Ireland. It is also the sector most at risk – in both jurisdictions – from Brexit. In the south, it faces restrictions and costs in accessing its major export market, GB. In the north, it faces the loss of Common Agricultural Policy support and uncertainty over the extent through any replacement support scheme. It should be remembered that some advocates for Brexit argued that leaving the EU created opportunities to eliminate farming support payments, sourcing food on the global market.

Farmers on both sides of the border must continue to be provided with CAP-style support. But state finance should not be a substitute for fair prices paid by wholesalers and retailers for food. Farming businesses in both Irish jurisdictions already faced challenges, even before Brexit, with supermarket chains using market power to buy cheaply, often at below the cost of production. The protection of farmers from unfair exploitation is required.

The creation of an all-island National Food Ombudsman would provide legally enforceable protection for primary producers and ensure fairness and equity in the food supply chain. There must be greater transparency in the food supply chain, breaking the hold of a small number of players. This would strengthen food security, while retaining the practice of family farming.

Brexit represents one of the biggest ever risks to farmers and the agri-food sector in Ireland, on both sides of the border. The food and beverage sector is the base of much of the rural economy, potentially causing severe damage in terms of new regional disparities. The agri-food sector provides over 250,000 jobs in rural communities in Ireland and is badly exposed to a negative Brexit.

More than a quarter of million people work in the agri-food sector in the south, with more than a third of Irish food exports going to the UK. The sector is particularly important to the rural economy, with only about a fifth of the sector's employment being based in Dublin. It is essential that Northern Ireland remains fully integrated into the EU's Single Market, without restrictions (including extra costs) in selling to either the EU or GB. State financial intervention may be needed in both jurisdiction to deal with some restructuring caused by Brexit.

It is important that production subsidies are simple to administer, reducing the burden on farming businesses while strengthening protection against fraud by more effective use of data analysis. Support payments need to be geared increasingly to carbon reduction targets, so protecting the environment and organic farming methods, while encouraging the adoption of productive systems. We need to develop a balance in rural areas, supporting a new generation of farmers by offering them a sustainable and rewarding future. This involves specific measures to support the beef, dairy and sheep sectors, to ensure their continuing viability.

HOUSING

Housing policy in the Republic needs reform, as it is clearly failing people because of its unaffordability for many. More apartments need to be built in Irish cities, with institutional investors taking a leading role in increasing the provision of properties for rent. Increased supply can be expected to lead to lower costs.

In Northern Ireland, more apartment development should also be welcomed. Attempts at creating shared housing have been constrained because the focus has been on houses rather than apartments. Shared housing estates have been subject to conflicting attempts by sectarian paramilitary groups to exercise control and 'ownership'. City centre apartment developments organically create shared housing environments, that are unlikely to be subject of attempts by paramilitary groups to exercise control in ways that have blighted attempts to construct housing developments in Northern Ireland.[223]

The adoption by the Central Bank of Ireland of new rules requiring higher deposits has made it more difficult for young families to own their own homes. The need for higher deposits reflects a more cautious approach, to avoid a repetition of the 2008/9 crisis, in which property prices spiralled down. A more European approach to properties – with an increased percentage of homes being rented in place of home ownership – should be encouraged. Rent controls are common in continental Europe and any increase in the construction of apartments should be accompanied by effective regulation to protect the interests of tenants, ensuring their financial rights are protected and that living conditions are good.

Housing associations should be encouraged to lead the development of mixed tenure estates in both jurisdictions, attracting finance from institutional investors. This would assist with social integration, finance a greater number of properties for social rent and provide good returns for pension providers.

A greater provision of affordable housing is essential not only for the social welfare of citizens across the island of Ireland, but also for economic development. The lack of affordable housing in Ireland is a significant barrier to new investment.

A properly financed programme for shared housing needs to be put in place in Northern Ireland, with the objective of greatly increasing the provision of high quality, safe, affordable, shared housing provision.

CRIMINAL JUSTICE

Cross-border crime is a growing challenge. The impact of a failure to adequately provide a cross-border policing response is evident in the events at the Quinn empire that operated across the Fermanagh/Cavan border. International smuggling of people and of drugs by border criminals has also been facilitated by the challenges encountered by two police forces operating separately.

These cases has made clear the need for greater co-operation between Garda Siochana and the PSNI. In the longer term, these two forces should merge to eliminate the ability of criminals to evade detection and monitoring. In the short-term it makes sense for cross-border task forces to operate that draw in members from both police services and improve the collection and sharing of information.

Drug gangs operate across borders, sometimes with impunity. Both they and vehicle thieves use the border to evade policing. This is clearly unacceptable and also breaches an important principle of equity – people and businesses located near the border have a poorer policing service than those located elsewhere. Fisheries protection officers operate on a cross-border basis, so there appears to be no objection in principle to cross-border enforcement operations.[224]

As well as addressing the problems of cross-border crime gangs, better cross-border co-operation by the two police services is also required to address sexual crime. It has become evident that similar sexual offences have been conducted by the same people in both Donegal and Fermanagh. It is to be hoped that detection has not been held back by any lack of sharing of information and forensic evidence. In addition, it makes sense in economic regions that cross borders – such as Derry-Letterkenny and Newry-Dundalk – to consider the sharing of victim support facilities, such as rape crisis centres.

Illegal waste dumping is a specific problem facilitated by the border. The environmental, financial and fiscal impacts of illegal waste disposal should not be underestimated. The Mobouy site near Derry is believed to be the largest illegal dump in Europe, facilitating more than £10m of landfill tax evasion. Instead, taxpayers are likely to have to spend tens of millions of pounds to remediate a dangerous site. It is believed that some of the waste illegally dumped on the site came from Donegal. Meanwhile some of the illegal wastes dumped in Donegal originated in Northern Ireland. The scale and the impact of this 'illegal industry' demonstrate the opportunities for a single cross-border environmental protection agency, with powers of investigation and arrest.

ENVIRONMENTAL PROTECTION

Ireland has the opportunity to be a world leader in environmental protection, which would not only provide an example of political ethics, but also create important economic development opportunities. It is already a leader in the use of wind energy, but needs to do more in taking advantage of natural resources favouring wave, hydro and tidal energy.

Existing applications in Northern Ireland at Rathlin Island and Strangford Lough are indications of how the tidal sector might be expanded.

But environmental protection means more than developing renewable energy provision, the establishment of a comprehensive electric vehicle recharging network and ending illegal waste dumping. We also need to invest in an effective circular economy, in which most of our wastes are instead seen as resources to be reused. This sector requires investment, backed by higher education R&D. It is essential that this R&D draws on best practice across EU institutions – a situation now much easier for universities in the Republic than those in Northern Ireland because of Brexit. Waste reuse targets need to be backed by legislation and investment. While the polluter pays principle is important, it needs to be recognised that creating perverse financial incentives to dump or burn waste is counter-productive. The system of rates payments used in Northern Ireland that provide free rubbish collection – with wastes sorted between recyclable and non-recyclable rates – is more sustainable than the system currently used in the Republic for households to pay for rubbish disposal.

The rural character of the island of Ireland creates challenges for the provision of a comprehensive and affordable public transport system. Yet it is important that public transport is an available and affordable alternative to private car ownership. It is also important that the planning system promotes urban living, preventing rural sprawl with isolated dwellings separated from the utilities network and public transport provision. A single public transport system for the whole island is needed, with integrated smart ticketing, expansion of the rail network and investment in the Belfast-Dublin rail line to create fast, hourly services. The expansion of the rail network to more areas of the west is desirable.

Cycling must be a safe alternative to private and public transport options, as an environmentally sustainable, cheap and healthy mode of travel. Investment in cycle networks can lead to a range of social benefits, including improved long-term public health outcomes.

EDUCATION

Northern Ireland's education system is often lauded as one of the best in the world – yet that is mostly true for those who go to the highest performing grammar schools. The system is very geared to class and privilege, with clear evidence that pupils from poorer families are much less likely to go to grammar schools and much less likely to achieve good examination results and places at university.

Reform is required of Northern Ireland's education system, to reduce the number of school leavers without basic skills and to increase the provision of university places to improve the skills base in the labour market and to strengthen the sustainability of the economy and social structures. That reform should be based on the adoption of the Republic's education system, which is truly world leading. Overheads in Northern Ireland need to be cut, through a review of school provision, school mergers, expanded integrated provision and more sharing of resources between schools.

Where the Republic – as well as Northern Ireland – can improve and strengthen its provision is with apprenticeships. The whole island is behind the best practice demonstrated in much of the EU, and this may be a factor in lower levels of productivity amongst Irish SMEs compared to that in the FDI sector. It is important that poorer students have access to financial support to enable them to access opportunities for degrees and career opportunities.

SOCIAL INTEGRATION

The Republic of Ireland has become a socially inclusive and socially liberal country, though still marked by episodes of violent and abusive racism that are unacceptable. Citizens of all religions and none and of all ethnicities are treated with equality. The state, including the Garda, must act decisively against all episodes of racism, including to protect public services personnel.

Northern Ireland faces a bigger challenge in moving towards social inclusivity and social liberalism. Change must be a gradual process. The Assembly and Executive needs to recognise both minority and majority rights – the adoption of a Bill of Rights would be an important step towards this.

Some paramilitary groups remain active and some of these harbour very negative and poisonous racist attitudes. Other paramilitary groups are involved in using their positions of strength to manipulate and exploit members of ethnic minority communities, in breach of their civil rights and to engage in illegal activities. More must be done to combat these activities. As these paramilitary groups operate on a cross-border basis, it is essential that the two police forces co-operate on a structural and systematic basis. Paramilitaries are exploiting the partition of Ireland, characterised as the partition in policing.

Victims of persecution need protection – and that applies both to those who are being persecuted within Ireland and those reaching Ireland to escape persecution. More needs to be done to protect asylum seekers, to welcome them and to protect places of refuge for them. It is unacceptable that buildings identified as centres of protection should be subject to arson attacks. Asylum seekers should be integrated within our society as quickly as possible, including with the right to work, earn and pay taxes. Hate crime legislation needs to be strengthened, to ensure members of ethnic minorities, asylum seekers, women and members of the LGBTQ+ communities are protected, with the full backing of the law and the police.

PROTECTING THE GOOD FRIDAY AGREEMENT

It is essential to protect the Belfast / Good Friday Agreement. But perhaps it would be more honest to say the focus should be on implementing it. More than two decades after it was signed and agreed by public plebiscite, in many ways there has been a lack of wholehearted implementation.

Some senior unionists admit in private that in government they were focused on getting the better of Sinn Féin and had no commitment to working in genuine partnership. Similarly, some republicans admit in private – and some even in public – that they have no intention of helping Northern Ireland to work, which they believe would be counter-productive to the unity project. Both attitudes hold Northern Ireland society back.

Cross-border planning has never achieved as much as its advocates hoped. Examples can be seen in infrastructure development, economic development, tourism promotion and the sharing of health services. If joint promotion of border tourism locations is seen as too political contentious to make serious progress, what hope is there for cross-border policing integration?

Nor does the fault lie solely with the Northern Ireland Executive – and the absence of it for long periods. The UK government was rumoured to be obstructive when Derry City and Strabane District Council sought to put forward its City Deal as a partnership project with neighbouring Donegal County Council. To have a City Deal that ignores the cross-border character of travel to work and labour market areas means the programme will achieve less than it might have done.

Had the UK not left the EU, continued European funding would have been guaranteed for border projects. It is essential that similar funding streams are underwritten by the UK government.

But we also need much greater clarity and commitment to other elements of cross-border development. Existing cross-border bodies need to be supported, through greater genuine commitment by all three governments. But a mechanism is required to address issues where progress is inadequate, which might include referral to an independent arbiter.

What is also true is that there needs to be clarity over the future. The work of the Constitution Unit and universities in preparing the potential wordings of referendums and the composition of their electorates is enormously important and significant. But other matters also need to be clarified in advance – which include those matters that will need to be resolved at inter-governmental level, such as pension liabilities. These might also be considered by independent academic study in advance of referendum preparation.

Another matter of significance is the proposal for the election of future Irish presidents to be open to all adult Irish citizens, including those who reside and were born in the north. This is a clear recognition of the Irish state's responsibility for those in the north who identify as Irish. This might be supported by greater representation of the north in the Senate.

It would be helpful if the Oireachtas could move beyond its already important work of the Good Friday Implementation Committee, by establishing – preferably jointly with the Northern Ireland Assembly – A Commission for a New Ireland. This could operate in tandem with the proposed Citizens' Assembly to consider Irish unity.

This programme must be recognised as a serious challenge for unionists, or the Ulster British as we can perhaps refer to them instead. It is asking more unionists to recognise that Irish society is changing, north and south, and will change even more. This is the result not just of demography, but also of the strategic failure of part of unionism in supporting and advocating for Brexit.

But this programme also represents as big a challenge for republicans. It is not acceptable for republicans – whether in Sinn Féin, the Irish Republic Socialist Party or in one of the dissenting republican groups – to claim that they are the only legitimate voice for Irish unity. Instead, they will have to recognise that unity can only be achieved through a majority vote in which large numbers of former unionists become supporters of Irish unity. And that can only happen if unity is separated from the history of violent republicanism.

If, though, it is unacceptable for physical force republicanism to be at the forefront of the debate for Irish unity, it is equally unacceptable for some in unionism to argue that Irish unity must be rejected solely because of past IRA campaigns.

The future needs to be non-violent. It requires open minds and a new beginning. It requires a new Ireland.

14
A BILL OF RIGHTS

THE BELFAST Agreement (Good Friday Agreement) makes several references to a potential Bill of Rights for Northern Ireland, as well as compliance with the European Convention on Human Rights. It should be noted that former prime minister Theresa May and her successor Boris Johnson have indicated their willingness to remove the UK from the remit of the ECHR.

The Belfast Agreement says: "The new Northern Ireland Human Rights Commission will be invited to consult and to advise on the scope for defining, in Westminster legislation, rights supplementary to those in the European Convention on Human Rights, to reflect the particular circumstances of Northern Ireland, drawing as appropriate on international instruments and experience. These additional rights to reflect the principles of mutual respect for the identity and ethos of both communities and parity of esteem, and - taken together with the ECHR

- to constitute a Bill of Rights for Northern Ireland. Among the issues for consideration by the Commission will be: "the formulation of a general obligation on government and public bodies fully to respect, on the basis of equality of treatment, the identity and ethos of both communities in Northern Ireland"; and "a clear formulation of the rights not to be discriminated against and to equality of opportunity in both the public and private sectors."

The agreement also says: "There will be safeguards to ensure that all sections of the community can participate and work together successfully in the operation of these [devolved] institutions and that all sections of the community are protected, including..... arrangements to provide that key decisions and legislation are proofed to ensure that they do not infringe the ECHR and any Bill of Rights for Northern Ireland".

"The Assembly may appoint a special Committee to examine and report on whether a measure or proposal for legislation is in conformity with equality requirements, including the ECHR/Bill of Rights."

"The Assembly will have authority to pass primary legislation for Northern Ireland in devolved areas, subject to: (a) the ECHR and any Bill of Rights for Northern Ireland supplementing it which, if the courts found to be breached, would render the relevant legislation null and void".

It is clear from these references that the signatories supported the creation of a Bill of Rights for Northern Ireland and expected one to be enacted. However, there is no Bill of Rights for Northern Ireland.

A substantial consultation document on a Bill of Rights for Northern Ireland was published in September 2001 by the Northern Ireland Human Rights Commission, yet did not lead to legislation.

While the St Andrews Agreement amended various aspects of how government operated in Northern Ireland, it did not attempt to remove the apparent commitment to a Bill of Rights. Indeed, it contained a promise to act in furtherance of the Bill of Rights.

The St Andrews Agreement says: "The Government will continue to actively promote the advancement of human rights, equality and mutual respect. In the pursuit of which we commit to the following: .... We will establish a forum on a Bill of Rights and convene its inaugural meeting in December 2006."

The Northern Ireland Human Rights Commission's Forum produced recommendations in December 2008, but the Forum itself was boycotted by both the DUP and the Catholic Church. Both rejected the outcome because of their position opposing abortion, which was not accepted by the Forum.

The Forum recommended that a Bill of Rights for Northern Ireland should include rights supplementary to the ECHR, including socio-economic rights, children's rights and environmental rights, as well as broadening the definition of a 'victim'. The Northern Ireland Office rejected the majority of the NIHRC's recommendations on the basis that the rights were not specific to the circumstances of Northern Ireland as required by the terms of reference and that they might be more appropriately addressed as part of the debate over a UK Bill of Rights.

The Northern Ireland Human Rights Commission continues to support the adoption and implementation of a Bill of Rights for Northern Ireland.

A model draft Bill of Rights for Northern Ireland has been produced by the Transitional Justice Institution, an Ulster University research institute.[225]

15
REVIEWING THE BELFAST/ GOOD FRIDAY AGREEMENT

THE OPENING declaration of the GFA said:

> 1. "We, the participants in the multi-party negotiations, believe that the agreement we have negotiated offers a truly historic opportunity for a new beginning."
>
> 2. "The tragedies of the past have left a deep and profoundly regrettable legacy of suffering. We must never forget those who have died or been injured, and their families. But we can best honour them through a

fresh start, in which we firmly dedicate ourselves to the achievement of reconciliation, tolerance, and mutual trust, and to the protection and vindication of the human rights of all."

3. "We are committed to partnership, equality and mutual respect as the basis of relationships within Northern Ireland, between North and South, and between these islands."

The GFA stated that the two governments -

(v) "affirm that whatever choice is freely exercised by a majority of the people of Northern Ireland, the power of the sovereign government with jurisdiction there shall be exercised with rigorous impartiality on behalf of all the people in the diversity of their identities and traditions and shall be founded on the principles of full respect for, and equality of, civil, political, social and cultural rights, of freedom from discrimination for all citizens, and of parity of esteem and of just and equal treatment for the identity, ethos, and aspirations of both communities;"

(vi) "recognise the birthright of all the people of Northern Ireland to identify themselves and be accepted as Irish or British, or both, as they may so choose, and accordingly confirm that their right to hold both British and Irish citizenship is accepted by both Governments and would not be affected by any future change in the status of Northern Ireland."

Despite the positive intentions of the Good Friday Agreement, it is clear that it is not perfect. Implementation has been problematic. And the Agreement does not reflect some changes in Northern Ireland society, particularly the demographic change towards a more mixed, less religious, society.

The most recent (2018) Northern Ireland Life and Times Survey[226] found 17% of respondents described themselves as having "no religion", compared to 39% Catholic, and 15% each for Church of Ireland and Presbyterian. In addition, 1% were Free Presbyterian, 4% Methodist, 1% Baptist, 1% Pentecostal, 1% other Protestant and 1% Muslim. Moreover, while 26% of respondents described themselves as unionist and 21% as nationalist, some 50% of respondents considered themselves neither unionist nor nationalist. (Strangely, 2% said they didn't know and another 1% had a view noted as "other".)

These results strongly suggest that the Assembly's system of political designation for members as 'nationalist', 'unionist' or 'other' has become inappropriate and outdated. It may also be a factor in the low voter turnout in elections.

The principles of civic engagement should also be reviewed. While the Civic Forum fell into disuse – with disdain expressed by the main unionist and republican parties – the New Decade New Approach framework includes reference to civic consultation mechanisms being used once or twice a year. The success of the Citizens' Assembly in the Republic suggests a more successful model that could be built into the workings of the Good Friday Agreement and the Assembly in the future.

Further, there can be little optimism about the Assembly and Executive institutions proving durable, given the frequent difficulties and suspensions that have been experienced. A consensus may need to be established about future arrangements should the institutions fail again. One option that has been floated is to provide measures that more effectively demand ministers act in compliance with the intentions of the GFA, possibly backed up by judicial review.

It is clear that cross-border bodies need to be strengthened and used more effectively as a means to achieve improved efficiencies and lower costs. An example is the opportunity to reduce duplication in tourism promotion, through the complete merger of existing agencies. Another instance is provided by the more effective operations of IDA compared to Invest NI.

It would also be helpful if there could be more effective joint planning across the two jurisdictions, including shared budgets, for transport projects, including roads. There are obvious examples where the current system causes problems through the lack of harmonisation: the high quality M1 from Dublin becomes a slower A1 road as it heads to Belfast; the A5 Derry-Dublin road has been subject to numerous delays of construction; and any possibility of a ring-road on the west side of Derry would have to involve repeated navigation of the border (as is already the case in roads in Co. Armagh and Co. Louth). As well as this, the border provides an unacceptable escape route and arbitrage opportunity for criminals – requiring a more effective method to achieve cross-border policing and prosecution.

These issues mean that greater commitment is required to both Strand Two and Strand Three of the GFA. Strand Two provides the basis for co-operation between the governments of Northern Ireland and the Irish government. This specifies: “Under a new British/Irish Agreement dealing with the totality of relationships, and related legislation at Westminster and in the Oireachtas, a North/South Ministerial Council to be established to bring together those with executive responsibilities in Northern Ireland and the Irish Government, to develop consultation, co-operation and action within the island of Ireland - including through implementation on an all-island and cross-border basis - on matters of mutual interest within the competence of the Administrations, North and South.”

It has not been possible for the North/South Ministerial Council to function without the Assembly and Executive themselves functioning. It is important not only that the Ministerial Council again meet now that the Assembly has resumed, but that ministers become genuinely committed to making the Ministerial Council effective. Joint work between the two authorities could be extremely advantageous to both, especially with the Brexit-imposed new trade arrangements. Some 146 areas of mutual co-operation were identified during the withdrawal negotiations.

Strand Three of the GFA has also been neglected. This provided for the British-Irish Intergovernmental Conference. This is supposed to bring together the British and Irish governments “to promote bilateral co-operation at all levels on all matters of mutual interest within the competence of both governments”. This takes place too infrequently: at the time of writing the last sitting of the conference was in May 2019, which specifically considered Brexit.

This would seem to breach the specific commitments entered into in Strand Three, which specify: "In recognition of the Irish Government's special interest in Northern Ireland and of the extent to which issues of mutual concern arise in relation to Northern Ireland, there will be regular and frequent meetings of the Conference concerned with non-devolved Northern Ireland matters, on which the Irish Government may put forward views and proposals. These meetings, to be co-chaired by the Minister for Foreign Affairs and the Secretary of State for Northern Ireland, would also deal with all-island and cross-border co-operation on non-devolved issues."

A further issue of serious concern relates to identity and citizenship. The GFA emphasises parity of esteem for the communities. It goes further by specifying that it "recognise[s] the birthright of all the people of Northern Ireland to identify themselves and be accepted as Irish or British, or both, as they may so choose, and accordingly confirm that their right to hold both British and Irish citizenship is accepted by both Governments and would not be affected by any future change in the status of Northern Ireland."

Yet the experience of Emma de Souza[227] and her spouse demonstrates that the legal meaning of this text is less than its apparent meaning – at least in the view of the Home Office. Emma has been unsuccessful in obtaining the right of her United States spouse to live with her as an Irish national, born in Northern Ireland. She must instead either seek permission for him to live in Northern Ireland by using the British citizenship that is obtained by her birthright, or else apply to renounce a British citizenship that she does not recognise.

The actions of the Home Office mean – unless the law is changed or Emma wins the next stage of the appeal process – that people born in Northern Ireland legally remain British citizens under UK law, even where they identify only as Irish. Many observers believe this is both perverse and a breach of the spirit of the GFA.

It is clear that aspects of the workings of the GFA require a review. One option would be for an all-island Citizens' Assembly to convene to review its workings.

16 PLANNING THE FUTURE

"WE NEED to achieve a meeting of minds, in ways that unite the people of Northern Ireland, and also unite the people of all of the island of Ireland," said Colm McKenna, a cross-border business entrepreneur, who is also the research co-ordinator of A New Ireland. "This should involve building on the experience of the Civic Forum in Northern Ireland and the Citizens' Assembly in the Republic. That might involve parallel forums, that bring out the concerns of different communities."

Colm argues: "It is essential to acknowledge that violence is wrong, unjustified and unnecessary in promoting a particular constitutional preference. It is also counter-productive and has made the case for Irish unity more challenging to make.

"Today, we have, happily, moved on. Those who share similar values should work together to shape the future. We can acknowledge that the interests of groups who come from different backgrounds are not mutually exclusive. To make progress towards that goal it is necessary to recognise that only non-violence will take us in the right direction and that progress can only be made by making Northern Ireland work, politically, socially and economically. Then we can all let the future take its course.

"It is not enough to achieve a united, new, Ireland. That is a starting point. We have to make the new nation work. Part of the foundations for that is to make Northern Ireland work as a place that is at ease with itself. We need to strive for a united people within what is now Northern Ireland.

"But these objectives are not easy to achieve and inclusive dialogue is a means of making progress. Those conversations need to include many of the themes considered within this book – education, health, economics, policing, identity, symbols. We need to consider how we accommodate each other. This should include not only having a Citizens' Assembly to consider our future relationships, but also how to embed this within our constitutional arrangements on a continuing basis.

"We neither can nor should jettison our past. Ireland's relationships with Britain go back a long way. We aim to remain friends. We hope that Britain will ease the way forward to our future. There will be permanent ties – perhaps membership of the Commonwealth, compromises over symbols of identity, continuation of the British-Irish Intergovernmental Conference and the British-Irish Council.

"We in Ireland should be confident enough of our future not to get too caught up in the past that it trips us up."

A CITIZENS' ASSEMBLY NOW?

More than a thousand well known Irish citizens from both sides of the border wrote to then Taoiseach Leo Varadkar at the end of 2019, calling for the Irish government to convene a Citizens' Assembly to consider Irish unification. Signatories included the economist David McWilliams, singer Christy Moore and actor Adrian Dunbar. Despite the support, the call was rejected by Varadkar.

Its organiser, Niall Murphy, a Belfast solicitor, said: "We need to plan for the future and the inevitabilities of demographic change and economic imperatives. We can't replicate the ill prepared recklessness of the Brexit referendum. We need to consult, converse, plan, and prepare for Ireland's future."

But Irish Times political correspondence Ronan McGreevy warned Murphy and the signatories: "In reality many in the Republic are hostile or indifferent to the proposition [of Irish unity]. The chasm in understanding between northern and southern nationalists is something that is rarely acknowledged, but if proponents of a united Ireland want an honest debate, they are going to have to have that discussion."[228]

Mick Fealty, editor of the Slugger O'Toole website, added his own characteristic note of caution. He wrote: "Belfast solicitor Niall Murphy, one of the founders of Ireland's Future, says that the open letter to Taoiseach Leo Varadkar 'represents a holistic overview of an island's view that we need to talk'. If so, where are the unionist signatories on it? A debate on a united Ireland which only seeks to agree with the proposition is not a debate at all. A citizens' assembly set up with a pre-ordained outcome in mind, in this case a united Ireland, is not what such forums are supposed to be about. A citizens' assembly is a courtroom not a parliament."[229]

Fealty regularly challenges arguments for Irish unity, so the tenor of his remarks is no surprise. But the point he makes is legitimate and represents a serious challenge for advocates of a united Ireland. As Denis Bradley has also observed, how do you have a conversation with someone who does not wish to talk? Fergus O'Dowd TD has similarly made the point that it is seriously difficult for the Irish government and Irish politicians to discuss an all-island approach to difficulties, when leading members of the DUP refuse to meet them.

Peter Robinson has argued that demographics mean that unionists can no longer adopt this attitude, but must instead now engage in the conversation of possible unity. Brexit represents not just a challenge to the status quo in Northern Ireland, but now means an inevitable change to the way people live and work.

Improving the workings of Strand Two of the Good Friday Agreement would certainly help with the atmosphere across the island of Ireland, as well as assist dealing with major challenges, such as health services reform and cross-border policing. The absence of adequate progress on these matters suggests that Strand Two is not taken sufficiently seriously.

Colin Harvey, professor of human rights at Queen's University, has become a prominent proponent of Irish unity, making a number of practical proposals on how to prepare for this. Colin has suggested referendum polls on unity should be held simultaneously on both sides of border on 22 May, 2023, the 25th anniversary of the referendum that ratified the Good Friday Agreement. He also suggests a way forward to improve relationships and to discuss a possible inclusive settlement.

Writing for the Eamonn Mallie website[230], Harvey asked how the conversation should proceed. Answering his own question, he said: "Firstly, it makes sense to bring clarity and certainty by agreeing a framework for the process. This would be a feasible thing for both governments to do as part of the current talks. Civic conversations will continue, and that is where the courageous work of societal transformation will happen, but an intergovernmental agreement would assist. This must build on the existing provisions of the Good Friday Agreement, and any attempt to revise those would be a mistake. No one on either side will be entirely pleased with a 50%+1 outcome, but that will suffice. The British Irish Intergovernmental Conference, following extensive consultation and engagement, could usefully set out the parameters on how this will be taken forward and led by both states.

"There seems to be broad agreement, for example, that a forum /assembly /convention should be established, informed by existing experience in Ireland. Is there any reason of principle, given the repeated emphasis on planning, why this cannot be established soon? I have made the case for setting out an agreed date. There are political and constitutional complications around this, but 22 May 2023 seems as good a date as any. It gives plenty of time for preparation, and pays due regard to the significance of that date for this island. Others can suggest alternatives, either sooner or later (Brexit may force earlier reflection). It is right that there is growing frustration with both governments about the need for precision and detailed proposals; naming a timeframe will help to address that. It will focus minds in a productive way.

"Secondly, this will at times be a challenging and uncomfortable conversation for everyone and that is a good thing. It will make all sides move beyond platitudes. Rather than construct this as an anxiety ridden democratic engagement why not view it through a radically different lens? This is a chance for an island-wide exercise in participatory democracy where there will be an opportunity to listen, learn and exchange ideas. We will know each other better at the far end. The island will be a better place afterwards, whatever the outcome. Unionism/loyalism will have to explain why remaining within the UK is the best way forward for this society; nationalism/republicanism must paint a convincing picture of what a united Ireland will offer. Both will have to reach beyond their own constituencies and speak persuasively to concerns not normally addressed. The onus is often placed on advocates of Irish unity to provide concrete assurances, but in the context of Brexit there is a heavy weight of responsibility on unionism to outline what will be done to make people feel respected, protected and secure in the existing constitutional arrangements. Will people opt for generosity or will fear prevail?

"Thirdly, there is no conflict between seeking rights-based power-sharing government in this region and arguing for constitutional change. That is precisely what the Agreement is intended to guarantee. The idea that those advancing the constitutional goal of Irish unity want to see people in this society humiliated and degraded within a disastrous political mess is offensive. Those arguing robustly for equality, rights and climate/social justice want this place to be more ambitious in the context of this island and these islands. Why, for example, return to an unreformed and flawed regime in order to perpetuate failure, legitimise sustained disrespect and manage socio-economic injustice? It is those who collude with policies of socio-economic devastation and who continually deny equality, rights and respect who are the real cheerleaders for systemic political failure here. Parties with 'unionist' in the title appear today as the greatest enemies of the current union, and those who appear least willing to defend the basic rights of members of their community.

"The utter silence over the appalling impact on unionist/loyalist communities of Brexit is remarkable (and it is only one example). This region can do so much better. People should not be fearful about advancing their equally legitimate political aspirations and seeking governance structures that respect the equality and rights-based vision of the Agreement.

"This constitutional conversation is happening and will continue. Rather than run away from it or pretend it can be avoided why not simply embrace it as an intrinsic part of our distinctive constitutional architecture. Bringing clarity and certainty to this is needed and will be welcome. If consent does genuinely underpin the status of this place then what precisely is the problem with testing it? Civic leadership is resilient and will persist, however, it is time for both governments and all political parties to move into a new phase."

Ultimately, it will be necessary to convene a special series of meetings of the British Irish Intergovernmental Conference to negotiate the outline of a possible deal on Irish unity. That outline arrangement would then need to be put to referendums on both sides of the border. If those two referendums both provide a positive vote, there would then be a new set of meetings of the Conference to finalise arrangements, including detail on finance, before a confirmatory referendum in each jurisdiction. (This type of process has been recognised as necessary by the research being led by the Constitution Unit.)

But at an earlier stage, there will need to be a civic conversation, which might be structured as a Citizens' Assembly. The question then is when it should take place, how it should be structured and who should convene it. We have reached a stage where such a debate cannot be delayed much longer. But unionist concerns may mean that the Irish government will not be seen as an honest broker in convening it (despite the lack of any indication from the main two Irish parties that they are keen to see Irish unity happening quickly).

Increasingly it is likely to be left to academics, and formally by universities, to take the initiative in making progress on these debates. Constitutional experts, including specialist lawyers, government advisors and economists will need to sit at the centre of these conversations, including outlines for a possible financial settlement between the two states post-Irish unity.

Until now, the narrative has been that Irish unity cannot be discussed with Brexit outstanding. However, the UK formally left the EU at the end of January 2020 and prime minister Boris Johnson has insisted that the transition period will not extend beyond the end of 2020. It seems sensible, on this basis, that universities and others make progress immediately on having the conversations around Irish unity.

A united Ireland, whatever it is called, is not imminent. But preparations for it should be.

CONCLUSION

"I CAN contemplate myself voting for a New Ireland if the economics were right and giving some identity for unionism. For someone whose grandfather was a unionist MP, and I served in the UDR myself, I've served Queen and country, to have shifted that far, is, when you think about it, it is quite a change."[231]

Those words of former Alliance Party MLA Will Glendinning are indicative of a change that is blowing across Northern Ireland – the extent and significance of which is only now beginning to be recognised.

We probably would by now have been closer to achieving Irish unity if it had not been for the Troubles and the campaign of violence. The fact that those who lived through the Troubles on the unionist side are the ones who are usually the most implacably opposed to Irish unity illustrates that. For these reasons it is essential that arguments for a united, new, Ireland now need to be objective and conciliatory, led by those with less history and more future.

Despite the wish of some, we will not be protesting ourselves into the future, only back into the past – a place no one should want to revisit.

Both the economic and social arguments for Irish unity are strong. The case for continued membership of the union with Britain are increasingly weak, with little apparent emotional commitment to it by the British government or the voters of England.

This book has presented the reasons for Irish unity. It is also provided a programme for unity, suggesting that it would be wrong to seek a 'big bang' all in one day transfer of sovereignty. Much needs to be done to heal Northern Ireland's society and economy – more than can be achieved simply by a change of constitutional jurisdiction.

A ten year framework is surely a sensible approach. It gives us time to make the economic changes that are needed. It is not without risks, but so is the alternative of trying to avoid change. Things cannot stay the same: a better outcome is possible.

APPENDIX ONE:
Ireland's Post Covid-19 New Order
Time to plan for the New Economic World Order

The outcome of this pandemic is unpredictable, but a few things seem likely:

- US dominance of the world will cease with China matching it;
- Globalisation as we know it will cease, but global trading continues, regionalisation will be the new norm, the EU will probably struggle through the Italian debt problem because Europe has been proven stronger together;
- We will change our priorities to secure production of what is essential for us to live;
- Technology will be used to control our environment, travel and leisure, with restrictions accepted as normal;
- There will be a rapid phasing out of cash, changing our understanding of 'money';
- Policing will change as a result of what we have learned in lockdown;
- Voting will go online, pulled between populists trying to prevent certain groups voting and liberals looking for more frequent votes - referendums on major issues;
- Virtual democratic assemblies will become common and may prove more efficient;
- As the citizens of deprived areas of cities realise their areas are more dangerous from a health point of view, the threat of pandemics will cause a dilemma for city planners: climate change arguably requires us to live closer together since its more energy efficient, but threats from the virus (with second waves emerging) will require us to live at a distance apart;
- A new value system will evolve in western societies with the living wage / universal basic income concepts being the norm;
- Robotics and data analysis will be widely adopted, with infringement on rights being restricted but accepted;
- The role of the state will expand, including widespread if temporary nationalisations;

- There will be no return to a full normal in the absence of a medical cure or preventative measure for Covid-19;
- Widespread international travel will not commence for a long time, with massive disruption to many countries' economies.

WHAT MUST IRELAND DO?

Ireland produces four times more food than it consumes, while France is the third largest producer of food in the world - so Europe can feed itself. We are increasing output from renewable energy and have a vibrant pharma research base and industry.

We need to optimize the supply chain and ensure more agility so that more people can work more flexibly, ensuring that reducing the amount produced or changing the nature of production does not produce layoffs of employees.

Food, medicine and effective healthcare are the new essentials – politicians' survival will depend on securing these for people.

It is unlikely that restaurants and cafes will re-open in the short term. As they do reopen, there will be fewer of them. People have become accustomed to shopping online for groceries and fashion items, so it is likely that 50% or more of high street shops and out of town retail centres will close.

The positive news is that we don't need to deal with Amazon to go online: many local shops are doing it for themselves and cutting out the middle person: this will save many of our more entrepreneurial business and may help them thrive.

To make up for the tax losses, Amazon and other online retailers will have to pay more in taxes and this will make up for the governments the lost revenues from traditional retailers.

In six months, it will not be feasible to continue furloughing people, so we are likely then to see the emergence of different economic models being forced upon governments to prevent widespread social disruption.

Regionalisation will become dominant. Regions that dealt with Covid-19 differently will emerge as close trading and economic regions – emerging together from lockdowns and restarting their economies in a similar fashion.

The Asia Pacific region, including Australia, handled Covid-19 in the most effective way and will thus be likely to restart their economies along similar lines first. Continental Europe and the Republic of Ireland (and de-facto NI) handled Covid-19 in a consistent way and are likely to deal with de-escalating lockdown similarly.

The UK and US handled Covid-19 in a similar way and are at similar points in the curve and are therefore likely to follow similar political paths going forward.

It would seem therefore that the three emerging regional trade blocks that will emerge from Covid-19 will be US – UK, Asia Pacific/Australia, and Europe including Ireland. It is for NI to decide which region it will be part of, but the relative success of the Republic's strategy will bear on the north's decision-makers.

In order to prepare for regionalisation we need:

1 A skilled workforce
2 Power infrastructure
3 Digital infrastructure (urban and rural)
4 Physical Infrastructure
5 Robotics and Data Analysis Skills

Industry will need to be more flexible using further automation and artificial intelligence to improve the resilience of supply chains and to ensure that they are agile enough to change their productions from one type of market to another's` product needs.

A network will be required that enable smartphone apps that detect their wearer's pulse, blood pressure and core temperature, with these opertional in rural as well as urban areas

Pandemics have come and gone before. The pandemic of the 1850s killed 10,000 Londoners, but showed the necessity for London to have a modern sewer network thus enabling it to expand and thrive. Similarly, opportunities will present themselves in the wake of this disaster and we must identify them now and begin to prepare for the future.

Colm McKenna, Research co-ordinator, A New Ireland

APPENDIX TWO: Leadership

By Mr Justice Richard Humphreys

The following is a speech given at the 'Our Rights Our Future' conference in Newry in May 2019 and reproduced by permission.

I START with a caveat. This is not a political contribution, it is legal and academic. I'm neutral regarding republicanism, loyalism, nationalism, unionism, a united Ireland, a UK hard Brexit, a soft Brexit or indeed, no Brexit. These are all political questions. What I'm not neutral about are concepts such as accommodation, reconciliation, dialogue, compromise, human welfare, peace, constitutional stability and the rule of law. So whether there is to be constitutional change or no con constitutional change, my basic message is that accommodation is the way forward.

When discussing rights into the future, it's a big topic so I obviously can't discuss all aspects of it in a few minutes, but I can single two rights in particular; the right to self-determination and rights under the European Convention on Human Rights (ECHR).

The key to the Good Friday Agreement is the right to self-determination, not in terms of the people of Northern Ireland but for the people of Ireland as a whole, without external interference. The right to self-determination is to be exercised by a concurrent majority, North and South and 'majority' means 50% of the total valid poll, plus one vote.

That is central. It is absolutely clear in the Good Friday Agreement and consequent British law. There must be no room for ambiguity about that because ambiguity about the test can only lead to unrest, if not violence.

That doesn't of course mean that 50% + 1 would be the best possible outcome. It just means that it is a legally sufficient and decisive outcome. Jamie Bryson recently demanded a change to UK law to require a super-majority. Well, you'd expect that I suppose, but (1) it would be illegal in terms of international law, and (2) he didn't explain why it would be OK to allow a minority of people to determine the constitutional status of Northern Ireland.

Some commentators, such as Fintan O'Toole, who I greatly respect, referred to the 50%+1 test as crude tribal majoritarianism. Others use phrases such as sectarian headcount and so on. But these descriptions are not valid for two reasons.

Firstly, the Good Friday Agreement provides for the 50% + 1 purely as a constitutional tie-breaker. *All other rights protections* are balanced and are not dependent on the views of the majority, and would endure, even after unity.

Secondly, the cornerstone of the agreement is parity of esteem. That means unionism is not a superior concept to nationalism or *vice versa*. A nationalist vote is not worth less than a unionist vote. No unionist would say that a vote to remain in the union is not legitimate if passed by 50% plus 1, so the test for a united Ireland must be the same.

Sean Donlon, who I also greatly respect, used the phrase, "*unionist consent in the context of a united Ireland*", but there can be no such concept as unionist consent for a united Ireland. That is for one simple reason - there is no requirement for nationalist consent to a United Kingdom.

The authors of the penultimate edition of *Kelly's Constitution* mused that maybe majority means majority of those on the electoral register. That's nonsense obviously, and they have corrected that in the current edition. It's fairly obvious why that's nonsense if you give it a second's thought – it implies that a vote to remain in the UK wouldn't be binding if didn't reach a majority on the electoral register, so Northern Ireland would have to be in some limbo-like state that was not envisaged by the Good Friday Agreement. The issue of the test is too important for back of an envelope musings and could cause severe problems on the ground if there is any confusion about what the Good Friday Agreement actually means.

The Good Friday Agreement is very explicit about the status of the ECHR - it is to be made part of the law in both jurisdictions, North and South (incorporation in the South is referred to in a sideways manner as something to be considered but involving an at least equivalent protection to that in the North – that can only mean considered positively). The British Government is required to complete incorporation into Northern Ireland law of the European Convention on Human Rights (ECHR), with direct access to the courts, and remedies for breach of the Convention, including power for the courts to overrule Assembly legislation on grounds of inconsistency. The Irish Government must provide equivalent protection. There is much discussion of the possibility that once Brexit is over, there may be moves to de-incorporate the ECHR and replace with a British bill of Rights. Whether that complies with the Good Friday Agreement is a legal question and my analysis is that it would be a breach of the Good Friday Agreement unless there was a link to the Strasbourg convention itself, and its caselaw. There will be a need for vigilance as to the details of any such legislation if it is proposed.

The third point that I want to make relates to the areas where nationalism needs to stretch and challenge itself. When I debated with Professor Colin Harvey two months ago in Trinity College Dublin Law School, I referred to the need for nationalists to challenge other nationalists when they were not being inclusive. I didn't anticipate that within a few weeks the challenge would come in tragic circumstances in the form of open palms dipped in bright red paint.

Whether we are talking about violence, terrorism and murder, or whether we are talking about any words or actions that are inflammatory, nationalism and republicanism needs to be active in policing its own side of the fence and challenging anything said or done that fails to respect rights, not so much by unionists and the British Government, but by its own side. That is leadership; and leadership is about actions, not about holding office. Leadership can be given by anyone.

A fundamental point was made in the aphorism attributed to Mahatma Gandhi, although it's probably a paraphrase rather than verbatim: "*be the change you want to see in the world*". So if you want accommodation, be accommodating. If you want to be listened to, listen. So my message to civic nationalism would be to take any opportunity you can get at an individual, personal, or collective level to reach out to and engage with your unionist counterparts and those of the "other" affiliation who are prepared to talk; and engage in a spirit of listening and accommodation.

A related point – Northern Ireland has got to be made to work. If some people think that the idea is let the statelet fail and then have a border poll in which people will react against failure by nodding through a united Ireland, this is a seriously flawed perspective on a number of levels.

The most basic level is that Northern Ireland is not going away even in a United Ireland. A fundamental point of international law is that treaties are to be observed, and the exception for unforeseen situations is extremely limited. So the Good Friday Agreement continues in force even after unity, and unity is not an unforeseen situation because it is specifically provided for in the agreement itself. So that means continued devolved institutions, power sharing and rights protection per the agreement after Irish unity. A contrary view is that if a treaty isn't working out for us we can tear it up – The English Attorney General, Geoffrey Cox, seemed to be hinting at something not far from that about the backstop. Such a view would be fundamentally misconceived and has very negative implications for the rule of law. Again, eternal vigilance is the price of liberty.

That takes us on to the need for a more accommodating vision of a United Ireland. Certainly the "four green fields" idea is dead in the water under the Good Friday Agreement. So I would say take it easy on the rush to a border poll idea until nationalism has had a conversation with itself on what shape a united Ireland would have. There should be a role in that discussion for all nationalist parties, for civic nationalism, and for anyone of the unionist or other camps that are prepared to discuss it.

Going back to Gandhi's point, asking for a united Ireland would be a lot more credible if it was accompanied by a statement of the 10 things nationalism is prepared to do for your unionist fellow residents of the 6 counties, not what you are prepared to do mañana, post unity, but in the here and now. It's not for me to say what they should be, but I will mention one example, the Commonwealth, simply because people see it as challenging and don't want to hear it.

I'm not arguing that we be should re-joining, just that it's worth discussing. It doesn't involve accepting the Queen as head of state, contrary to urban myth. Anyway, can we try to ease off on the Brit-bashing and the Queen-bashing just a bit. The Queen is more Irish than most British people – indeed she's more Irish than a lot of Irish citizens. She has loads of Irish ancestors including Brian Boru. She has the Irish harp in her coat of arms. The British have a chequered colonial history in South Africa too, but post-apartheid South Africa is a member of the Commonwealth, Nelson Mandela attended the Commonwealth heads of government meeting, held every few years, so he was supportive, notwithstanding the British colonial history in his country. Indeed he came back to the following meeting, but Irish nationalism is apparently not prepared to follow the inclusive example of Mandela.

It's also important to remember that rights are reciprocal. Certainly, there is much sympathy in this room for Emma de Souza, but people may not be conscious that there are unionist Emma de Souzas out there too. For example, Northern Irish people of British identity have to some extent dilute that identity if they wish to fully participate in Irish society. If a unionist accepts appointment to the Seanad, for example, they thereby become an Irish citizen by operation of law. They don't have to apply for a passport, but they are treated as citizens. If they renounced their Irish citizenship, they would automatically forfeit their seat in the Seanad. A unionist if she or he lives South of the border can't vote in a referendum without becoming an Irish citizen by operation of law. I go back to my earlier point, what are the 10 things you are going to do for those of a British identity, right here, right now?

On the subject of leadership, leadership is also about language, the names we put on things, how we talk about the past, what we commemorate. There is a lot nationalism can do in that space to be accommodating, and remember, if you say five accommodating things but one thing that is not accommodating and inclusive, it's the negative thing people will remember, especially if they are suspicious to begin with, so be consistent.

Leadership is also about what we take offence at. My message to nationalists would be, don't be snowflakes, maybe try laughing it off, inflammatory comments don't have to be taken seriously, try to be the bigger person … just a suggestion.

Leadership, finally, is open to everyone in this sense. The biggest and bravest thing that nationalists can say individual and collectively to their representatives is, we don't have to win 5-0, we don't even have to win 3-0, we will settle for an honourable 1-1 draw. Sure, we are talking about rights, but don't paint yourself into a corner by making the fundamental mistake that if you define something as a right, then no compromise is possible; that totally misses the point about the progressive nature of society.

"Tis much better to do a little with certainty, & leave the rest for others that come after you". One of the greatest minds in world history, Isaac Newton, said that. Build what you can today and leave something for tomorrow to achieve.

Richard Humphreys is a judge of the High Court in Dublin. His book, Beyond the Border: The Good Friday Agreement and Irish Unity after Brexit is published by Merrion Press.

APPENDIX THREE: Considering Change

CONSTITUTIONAL AND cultural concerns have to be considered as part of the move towards Irish unity. These two lists provide ideas for discussion.

CONSTITUTIONAL CONSIDERATIONS

1 A Bill of Rights that includes respect for British identity across this island, including respect for the Royal family;
2 Respect for the marching traditions of both cultures, including Orange parades, but subject to an overriding consent by host communities;
3 The right for those born in Ireland to opt for Irish or British nationality, or both, including full citizenship and respect for identity, with full equality for Irish and British passports;
4 Review of government structures, including consideration of federated and confederated systems, and whether one parliament or two;
5 Police and other security forces to be drawn from local populations;
6 Parity of esteem for English and Irish, official recognition of Ulster Scots.
7 Equal recognition of Catholic, Protestant and other religions and their place in Irish society and guaranteed respect for their identities and independence;
8 Recognition in the constitution of the special relationship Ireland has with the UK, historically and culturally;
9 New flags, the anthem and other regional and national symbols should be agreed through discussion, with the objective of achieving consensus;
10 No redistribution of land.

CULTURAL CONSIDERATIONS

1 British citizens within a united island would vote subject to residency requirements as per the UK situation for Irish citizens.
2 Joining the Commonwealth (as a Republic).
3 Recognise the 12th July as a bank holiday in the Republic, as recommended by ICTU.
4 Ensure that judges in the new Republic are trained in the laws of Scotland as they are now in English law.
5 Symbols such as shamrocks, green, the harp and the Irish language should be retained and added to with the lambeg drum or Crown.
6 Flags might include elements of the Union Jack and tricolour.
7 A new national anthem, decided through a form of national consensus.
8 Scots Irish should be recognised.
9 Legal and constitutional protection for people who do not speak Irish.
10 Remove need for compulsory Irish from students, lawyers, etc.
11 Irish citizens permitted to be members of the Privy Council or hold a knighthood.
12 The House of Lords (or the UK Senate, after possible reform) to continue to include members who live in Northern Ireland, after reunification.
13 Review Catholic Church's role in the provision of state funded public services.
14 Recognition of the International Court of Justice as a protection of unionists' rights.
15 Appointment of an ombudsman if a federated structure is adopted, to ensure Stormont or other assembly/ies undertake functions as per law and the Good Friday Agreement.

APPENDIX FOUR:
A Positive Challenge to Northern Nationalists

WE THE undersigned desire a transparent and inclusive debate concerning rights, truth, equality and civil liberties and in so doing challenge assumptions that such values are not embedded within civic unionism, pluralism and other identities.

We are motivated by the desire to build a society for the betterment of everyone. This cannot happen when such a commitment is perceived as being vested in one community or political persuasion. We find it frustrating and puzzling that civic unionism, pluralists and other forms of civic leadership have been rendered invisible in many debates focused on rights and responsibilities. It has reduced our capacity to be heard and undermines the power of reconciliation to shift society away from stale and limiting notions of identity.

We have worked for peace and reconciliation and in so doing have had open and transparent engagement with civic nationalism. That has included recognition of the need for equality and most importantly the urgent need for polarised communities in Northern Ireland to reconcile and deal with barriers to a better future. To achieve this requires the recognition that withholding truth presents as such. This is not unique to any institution or section within our society but where it is a selective process, healing a pernicious and destabilising past remains as a challenge to us all.

Civic unionism and other identities are not resistant to claims of equality and full citizenship. These identities are central to the development of an authentically fair and tolerant society.

We wish to unite, not divide, and in encouraging transparency we call upon civic nationalism and others to engage with us in frank and fulsome debates about the many values and beliefs that are commonly shared and are vital to transforming the issues that we face.

Signed by 105 people, mostly from a unionist background.

APPENDIX FIVE:
Notes from Our Rights, Our Future conference, Canal Court Hotel, Newry, May 2019

THE CONFERENCE considered the steps necessary to bring together unionists with those who believe in Irish unity. Speakers included Irish Senator and former UFU President Ian Marshall and Mr Justice Richard Humphreys.

- We need to identify common goals, values and interests;
- The problems of young people on the Shankill Road and in North Dublin are the same: unemployment, health, lack of job opportunities, drug use - not problems with the Irish language;
- People in both communities feel abandoned: we need to present a realistic future for the island that can address social isolation and alienation;
- Most unionists are not radical conservatives, most are hard working, tolerant, law abiding citizens who respect their neighbours, whose views must be listened to, respected and taken on board;
- Unionists need to begin to say that which they value and what is important to them – the Queen, the Union Jack, red letter boxes? – and for those concerns to be accommodated;
- There needs to be a recognition that for many unionists, republicanism means an armalite and a balaclava;
- Pushing the Tricolour and Irish language, knocking Brits, creates resentment;
- A New Ireland must be an agreed future, that includes unionists;
- There needs to be a willingness to see things 'from the other side';
- There is a big attitudinal difference between generations;
- Those whose who believe 1921 was wrong should recognise that forced unity would be wrong;
- A discussion is needed, started by civic society;
- More difficult sets of problems have been solved;
- Let economists, lawyers, etc., look at unity and its effects and

then consider the challenges;

- Partition may never have happened if we had taken this route;
- We need to be citizens rather than subjects;
- Ireland's 'rainy day fund' could be the unity fund
- We need to listen to the fears and grievances of those losing identity.

Notes by Colm McKenna

APPENDIX SIX:
Countdown to Unity or Groundhog Day?
By Desmond Murphy, Senior Counsel

IN 2008 Richard Humphries authored a book entitled 'Countdown to Unity' in which he outlined in detail a possible path towards the unification of Ireland. Since then there has been only two other significant works on the topic: Mark Daly`s 'Brexit and the Future of Ireland' and Paul Gosling`s 'The Economic Impact of an All Island Economy'.

However, since the vote of the United Kingdom to leave the European Union in June 2016 and the possibility of border controls, the debate on the future of Northern Ireland has sharpened to a level where many northern nationalists with an almost millenarian fervour have espoused the belief that Irish unity is inevitable and if it cannot be obtained by persuasion, will be achieved by the demography of a catholic majority in Northern Ireland in the near future.

Two points need immediately to be made:

1 Nothing is inevitable in history: a single example will suffice: most educated Europeans on 27 June 1914 would have taken for granted the continuation of peace and prosperity of previous 100 years and could never have imagined destructive European wars within six weeks.

2 The second point is the danger of precedents. While German unification was largely successful and quick for specific reasons, the disintegration of Yugoslavia in the 1990s into multiple sectarian civil wars should make one ponder, especially as it was praised in the 1970s and 1980s as an alternative to capitalism and communism.

The period 2016 – 18 was discouraging in Northern Ireland. The Executive collapsed in 2017. However, even worse was the complete collapse of trust between the DUP and Sinn Féin, and the virtual elimination of smaller parties. There has been an explosion in twitter abuse: false news and deliberate attempts to rewrite the past.

It is inevitable that this position will infect Catholic and Protestant outlooks eventually, more importantly this abuse and bad faith given an inkling to what a referendum on the future of Northern Ireland would consist of. It would create a sectarian mobilization not ever seen in Irish history and would probably climax in one side or the other not accepting the result. It would eliminate any dissenting voices especially in the Protestant community and could easily trigger the disintegration of society. It would mean an inclusive constitutional conference impossible.

Humphries' optimism of 2008 that issues such as the Irish language or flags and anthems could be resolved now seems misplaced. The bitter dispute over an Irish language act in Northern Ireland in the past few years, and the flags protests of 2012, suggest that compromise is now impossible; this hope of confidence building measures by nationalist Ireland now seems remote and impractical. Equally given the present strident languages, it would appear impossible for any unionist to negotiate on any form of Irish unity prior to a referendum.

However, in all texts considered, hard questions are avoided: a few can be alluded to here:

- What will be form of the state: if it is an independent republic then unionism will have lost and indeed cannot exist.
- If that is so, what is the point of recognizing British identity. The essence of unionism in Northern Ireland is loyalty to the crown and monarchy and to historical sacrifices on their behalf. If those links are snapped, fuzzy promises about holding British passports will be meaningless.
- Where would power lie in the new state, and more importantly what would be the distribution of such power. Unionists / Protestants could not exercise effective resistance in a new state unless there were artificial protections at the centre of power.
- Humphries reliance on the Good Friday Agreement as a means of driving constitutional change (p152) or the hope that a forum of joint authority over 30 years (p205) would ease the transition now seems sadly misplaced. Neither government has shown any interest in using the Good Friday Agreement to provide constitutional change as stalemate in Northern Ireland has

> prevented even modest workings of devolved institutions, never mind ambitious plans for a joint authority.

So, we have reached 'Groundhog Day' where the parties in Northern Ireland are content to abuse one another and allow society to fray at the edges. Topics that might be discussed at a constitutional convention will remain a wish list.

It requires imagination to break the current short and long-term stalemate. One suggestion would be to have a small independent commission receive suggestions for a different Ireland and to put the final proposals to the people in referendum north and south.

It would be made clear that if these were rejected, the status quo would continue, the position being that, if accepted, it would be possible to have detailed discussions on implementation without the pressure from either community that betrayal was imminent. It will be a slow process, but at least it would offer a fresh start and avoid reigniting the sectarian conflict in an even broader morass than before.

FOOTNOTES:

[1] https://www.health-ni.gov.uk/publications/systems-not-structures-changing-health-and-social-care-full-report

[2] https://www.bloomberg.com/news/articles/2020-01-10/-170-billion-and-counting-the-cost-of-brexit-for-the-u-k

[3] Economists paint gloomy picture for the year ahead, Financial Times, 2nd January, 2020.

[4]https://assets.publishing.service.gov.uk/government/uploads/system/uploads/attachment_data/file/760484/28_November_EU_Exit_-_Longterm_economic_analysis__1_.pdf#page=12

[5] https://www.economistsforfreetrade.com/

[6] Why even better news than Wrightbus being saved would be a Brexit that doesn't threaten to annihilate our manufacturing sector, Belfast Telegraph, 14 October, 2019

[7] Interview with BBC tv, Newsline, 17 January, 2020

[8] https://www.nisra.gov.uk/statistics/economic-output-statistics/ni-composite-economic-index

[9] http://www.europarl.europa.eu/RegData/etudes/BRIE/2017/583116/IPOL_BRI(2017)583116_EN.pdf

[10] https://www.quora.com/What-is-the-difference-between-GDP-and-GVA-and-why-GVA-is-more-relevant

[11] https://www.ons.gov.uk/economy/grossdomesticproductgdp/bulletins/regionaleconomicactivitybygrossdomesticproductuk/1998to2018#main-points

[12] https://www.ons.gov.uk/economy/grossvalueaddedgva/bulletins/regionalgrossvalueaddedbalanceduk/1998to2017

[13] 'Will Brexit kill Thatcherism?', Financial Times, 31 January, 2020

[14] There were 881,000 people employed at the end of 2019, but the calculation is based on employment figures in 2016, when the earlier economic analysis was produced.

[15] https://www.ufuni.org/farming

[16] ibid

[17] https://www.daera-ni.gov.uk/news/poor-farm-prices-have-made-2019-difficult-year-farmers-poots

[18] http://www.europarl.europa.eu/unitedkingdom/en/ukevents/brexitstudies.html
The report cites Aidan Stennett (2016) 'The EU referendum and potential implications for Northern Ireland', Northern Ireland Assembly Research and Information Service Research Paper, NIAR 32-16, p.8.

[19] https://www.ft.com/content/cd9323b8-ad0e-11e7-beba-5521c713abf4

[20] http://www.irishnews.com/paywall/tsb/irishnews/irishnews/irishnews//business/2018/01/16/news/ni-agriculture-subsidies-to-fall-after-brexit-warns-report-1232572/content.html

[21] https://www.finance-ni.gov.uk/articles/european-structural-and-investment-fund-programmes-northern-ireland

[22] https://www.daera-ni.gov.uk/topics/grants-and-funding

[23] http://www.niassembly.gov.uk/globalassets/documents/raise/publications/2016-2021/2016/aera/6616.pdf

[24] ibid

[25] https://www.agriland.ie/farming-news/close-to-100-of-uk-farms-could-be-worse-off-after-brexit/

[26] https://www.economistsforfreetrade.com/wp-content/uploads/2017/09/Economists-for-Free-Trade-NME-Paper.pdf

[27] https://assets.publishing.service.gov.uk/government/uploads/system/uploads/attachment_data/file/684003/future-farming-environment-consult-document.pdf

[28] http://www.thedetail.tv/articles/the-eu-s-common-agricultural-policy-should-we-stay-or-should-we-go

[29] https://www.irishtimes.com/opinion/northern-ireland-and-the-tripadvisor-index-of-economic-vibrancy-1.3311077

[30] https://www.belfasttelegraph.co.uk/opinion/news-analysis/demographics-are-shifting-towards-a-united-ireland-we-must-have-a-plan-35865222.html

[31] https://aib.ie/content/dam/aib/investorrelations/docs/economic-research/irish-economy/irish-economic-updates/irish-economy-update-august-2016.pdf

[32] https://www.belfasttelegraph.co.uk/business/northern-ireland/economy-watch-just-how-different-are-the-two-economies-on-the-island-of-ireland-37233173.html

[33] https://www.cso.ie/en/releasesandpublications/ep/p-rsdgi/regionalsdgsireland2017/ee/

[34] https://www.ons.gov.uk/economy/grossvalueaddedgva/bulletins/regionalgrossvalueaddedincomeapproach/december2015#regional-nuts1-gva-estimates

[35] https://www.nisra.gov.uk/statistics/economic-output-statistics/gross-value-added

[36] http://www.cso.ie/en/releasesandpublications/er/elca/earningsandlabourcostsannualdata2016/

[37] www.nisra.gov.uk/sites/nisra.gov.uk/files/publications/4xu-NI-ASHE-Bulletin-2017.PDF

[38] https://ec.europa.eu/eurostat/statistics-explained/index.php/Wages_and_labour_costs

[39] https://www.cso.ie/en/statistics/earnings/earningsandlabourcosts/, using the mean average

[40] https://www.nisra.gov.uk/publications/ashe-headline-statistics-northern-ireland, links to Excel chart

[41] https://sluggerotoole.com/2018/03/26/is-northern-ireland-dramatically-poorer-than-the-republic/

[42] https://www.nisra.gov.uk/news/labour-market-report-january-2020

[43] https://www.cso.ie/en/statistics/labourmarket/monthlyunemployment/

[44] https://www.cso.ie/en/releasesandpublications/er/lfs/labourforcesurveylfsquarter32019/

[45] http://budget.gov.ie/Budgets/2020/Documents/Budget/The%20Inactive%20Working%20Age%20Population.pdf

[46] https://www.cso.ie/en/releasesandpublications/er/lfs/labourforcesurveyquarter22018/

[47] https://www.irishtimes.com/business/economy/booming-economy-attracting-new-influx-of-foreign-nationals-1.3610131?mode=sample&auth-failed=1&pw-origin=https%3A%2F%2Fwww.irishtimes.com%2Fbusiness%2Feconomy%2Fbooming-economy-attracting-new-influx-of-foreign-nationals-1.3610131

[48] https://www.ey.com/en_ie/transactions/ey-economic-eye-autumn-forecast-2019

[49] ibid

[50] http://www.oecdbetterlifeindex.org/countries/ireland/

[51] ibid

[52] https://www.cso.ie/en/releasesandpublications/ep/p-gpii/geographicalprofilesofincomeinireland2016/incomeinireland/

[53] https://ec.europa.eu/eurostat/statistics-explained/index.php/Wages_and_labour_costs#Net_earnings_and_tax_burden

[54] https://www.ucc.ie/en/media/academic/economics/documents/research/wp00-3.pdf

[55] http://www.assemblyresearchmatters.org/2017/06/14/goods-northern-ireland-export-much-worth-go/

[56] https://www.economics.ox.ac.uk/materials/working_papers/2828/150-final.pdf

[57] ibid

[58] https://www.ey.com/ie/en/issues/business-environment/ey-economic-eye-summer-2018

[59] https://www.centralbank.ie/publication/quarterly-bulletins/quarterly-bulletin-q4-2019

[60] EY Economic Eye, Winter 2017

[61] https://www.qub.ac.uk/research-centres/CentreforInternationalBordersResearch/Publications/WorkingPapers/MappingFrontiersworkingpapers/Filetoupload,175406,en.pdf

[62] http://ec.europa.eu/eurostat/tgm/table.do;jsessionid=4pG0W6-BXFtjhx_6IF_4G5YrzZ1qOnmk5Wt0GhuR6xUa-vPIeHwj!-1102445943?tab=table&plugin=1&language=en&pcode=tgs00026

[63] http://www.irishborderlands.com/index.html

[64] https://academic.oup.com/joeg/article-abstract/13/6/889/924921?redirectedFrom=fulltext

[65] http://blogs.lse.ac.uk/politicsandpolicy/britains-spatially-unbalanced-economy/

[66] https://www.britac.ac.uk/pubs/proc/files/98p035.pdf

[67] ibid

[68] ibid

[69] https://www.economy-ni.gov.uk/sites/default/files/publications/deti/irep-report.pdf

[70] http://www.niassembly.gov.uk/globalassets/documents/enterprise-trade-and-investment/inquiry—-corp-tax/research-papers/20150319-assembly-research—-ida-ireland.pdf

[71] https://www.idaireland.com/newsroom/ida-ireland-achieves-all-targets

[72] https://secure.investni.com/static/library/invest-ni/documents/annual-report-investni-2016-17.pdf

[73] https://secure.investni.com/static/library/invest-ni/documents/annual-report-investni-2018-2019.pdf

[74] https://www.irishtimes.com/news/politics/government-looks-to-push-closer-german-ties-ahead-of-brexit-1.3458515?mode=sample&auth-failed=1&pw-origin=https%3A%2F%2Fwww.irishtimes.com%2Fnews%2Fpolitics%2Fgovernment-looks-to-push-closer-german-ties-ahead-of-brexit-1.3458515

[75] https://www.bbc.co.uk/news/uk-northern-ireland-51188910

[76] U4D, https://www.londonderrychamber.co.uk/.../1403886149—U4D—-need-to-increase-graduates

[77] U4D, ibid.

[78] U4D, ibid.

[79] https://www.pwc.co.uk/who-we-are/regional-sites/northern-ireland/press-releases/northern-ireland-productivity-amongst-lowest-in-the-developed-world.html

[80] https://www.ulster.ac.uk/__data/assets/pdf_file/0008/118385/Understanding_productivity_in_Northern_Ireland_27_September_2016.pdf

[81] https://www.nerinstitute.net/download/pdf/industrial_policy_wp_2016_061216.pdf

[82] https://www.ons.gov.uk/economy/economicoutputandproductivity/productivitymeasures/bulletins/internationalcomparisonsofproductivityfinalestimates/2016

[83] https://www.ons.gov.uk/employmentandlabourmarket/peopleinwork/labourproductivity/articles/regionalandsubregionalproductivityintheuk/february2018

[84] https://www.ons.gov.uk/employmentandlabourmarket/peopleinwork/labourproductivity/articles/regionalandsubregionalproductivityintheuk/jan2017#results-for-england-scotland-wales-and-northern-ireland-by-nuts3-subregions

[85] http://www.niassembly.gov.uk/globalassets/documents/raise/publications/2015/del/5415.pdf

[86] The ONS Productivity Handbook

[87] Northern Ireland competiveness damaged by graduate skills shortage, U4D

[88] https://www.nerinstitute.net/download/pdf/industrial_policy_wp_2016_061216.pdf

[89] http://eprints.lincoln.ac.uk/7652/1/u4dreportlow-res.pdf

[90] https://www.enterpriseresearch.ac.uk/wp-content/uploads/2016/05/GEM-UK-2015-final-report.pdf

[91] https://www.fsb.org.uk/docs/default-source/Publications/the-contribution-of-small-businesses-to-northern-ireland.pdf?sfvrsn=1

[92] https://www.fsb.org.uk/docs/default-source/Publications/the-contribution-of-small-businesses-to-northern-ireland.pdf?sfvrsn=1

[93] 'Northern Ireland Assembly must make immediate progress on urgent issues', Sunday Business Post, 12 January, 2020

[94] https://www.irishtimes.com/business/economy/john-fitzgerald-north-remains-land-of-lost-opportunities-1.3270295

[95] https://www.parliament.uk/business/committees/committees-a-z/commons-select/northern-ireland-affairs-committee/news-parliament-2015/electricity-sector-report-published-16-17/

[96] http://www.ibec.ie/IBEC/Press/PressPublicationsdoclib3.nsf/vPages/Newsroom~ibec-cbi-set-out-ambitious-plan-for-all-island-economy-24-07-2016?OpenDocument?OpenDocument

[97] http://isni.gov.uk/PDFs/Investment%20Strategy.pdf

[98] https://www.niauditoffice.gov.uk/sites/niao/files/226718%20NIAO%20Major%20Capital%20Projects_FINAL%20LW%20RES%20Complete.pdf

[99] https://www.per.gov.ie/en/national-development-plan-2018-2027/

[100] https://fullfact.org/europe/irish-border-trade/

[101] http://www.assemblyresearchmatters.org/2017/06/14/goods-northern-ireland-export-much-worth-go/

[102] http://www.bbc.co.uk/news/uk-politics-42223732

[103] https://fullfact.org/europe/irish-border-trade/

[104] https://fullfact.org/europe/irish-border-trade/

[105] http://www.assemblyresearchmatters.org/2017/06/14/goods-northern-ireland-export-much-worth-go/

[106] Department for the Economy briefing on Brexit

[107] Department for the Economy briefing on Brexit

[108] http://www.assemblyresearchmatters.org/2017/06/14/goods-northern-ireland-export-much-worth-go

[109] http://www.assemblyresearchmatters.org/2017/06/14/goods-northern-ireland-export-much-worth-go

[110] https://www.irishtimes.com/opinion/a-united-ireland-would-be-worse-off-than-the-republic-1.3010177

[111] https://www.tcd.ie/Economics/TEP/2019/tep0619.pdf

[112] https://www.esri.ie/system/files/publications/OPEA173.pdf

[113] http://prcg.com/modeling-irish-unification/report.pdf

[114] http://www.euronews.com/2018/02/05/how-fall-of-the-berlin-wall-paved-way-for-germany-s-populists

[115] https://www.irishtimes.com/business/economy/john-fitzgerald-north-remains-land-of-lost-opportunities-1.3270295

[116] A New History of Ireland, edited by JR Hill

[117] https://www.joe.ie/news/i-foresee-a-united-ireland-at-some-point-in-the-future-says-leo-varadkar-557422

[118] https://www.independent.ie/breaking-news/irish-news/simon-coveney-would-like-to-see-a-united-ireland-in-his-political-lifetime-36347866.html

[119] https://www.bbc.co.uk/news/world-europe-49127616

[120] https://www.bbc.co.uk/news/uk-northern-ireland-50104226

[121] https://www.politico.eu/article/united-ireland-after-brexit-reunification-vote/

[122] https://www.ucl.ac.uk/constitution-unit/research/elections-and-referendums/working-group-unification-referendums-island-ireland

[123] https://www.irishtimes.com/news/ireland/irish-news/a-united-ireland-could-need-four-referendums-says-expert-1.4016125

[124] 'Group Status, Conflict and National Identity: Evidence from Brexit in Northern Ireland', PhD paper

[125] https://pureadmin.qub.ac.uk/ws/portalfiles/portal/162207676/Hayward_McManus_Neither_Nor_paper_accepted_version.pdf

[126] 'Far from enjoying the best of both words, Brexit traps Northern Ireland between a rock and a hard place', Belfast Telegraph, 4 February, 2020

[127] UCD conference, 2019, as noted by Colm McKenna

[128] https://www.belfasttelegraph.co.uk/news/northern-ireland/peter-robinson-some-refuse-to-talk-about-the-elephant-in-the-room-but-it-is-positioning-itself-to-squat-upon-their-laps-37179957.html

[129] 'A United Ireland', by Kevin Meagher, published by Biteback Publishing, p.297

[130] http://cain.ulst.ac.uk/events/peace/docs/dsd151293.htm

[131] https://www.belfasttelegraph.co.uk/news/northern-ireland/theresa-mays-keynote-address-at-belfasts-waterfront-hall-full-speech-37138123.html

[132] A united Ireland would be good for everyone, Matthew Parris, The Times, 18 January, 2020

[133] https://www.belfasttelegraph.co.uk/news/northern-ireland/some-unionists-would-prefer-united-ireland-to-brexit-says-powell-36786960.html

[134] http://www.irishnews.com/paywall/tsb/irishnews/irishnews/irishnews//news/northernirelandnews/2019/12/17/news/brexit-could-lead-to-united-ireland-in-a-decade—1792498/content.html

[135] Interview by the author, see above

[136] https://www.cso.ie/en/releasesandpublications/er/pme/populationandmigrationestimatesapril2016/

[137] https://www.cso.ie/en/releasesandpublications/ep/p-cp7md/p7md/p7anii/

[138] https://www.cso.ie/en/media/csoie/releasespublications/documents/population/2017/Chapter_5_Diversity.pdf

[139] https://www.ninis2.nisra.gov.uk/public/Theme.aspx?themeNumber=136&themeName=Census%202011

[140] https://www.irishcentral.com/roots/history/ireland-ended-its-ban-on-divorce-19-years-ago-today

[141] https://www.irishcentral.com/roots/history/ireland-ended-its-ban-on-divorce-19-years-ago-today

[142] https://www.theguardian.com/world/2015/may/23/gay-marriage-ireland-yes-vote

[143] https://www.theguardian.com/world/2015/may/23/gay-marriage-ireland-yes-vote

[144] http://www.catholicherald.co.uk/issues/catholic-herald-app-2018-06-22/will-irelands-catholic-hospitals-defy-varadkar/

[145] The State of Housing in the EU, published by Housing Europe

[146] https://www.catholicireland.net/taoiseach-opens-first-new-catholic-secondary-school-30-years/

[147] https://www.thetablet.co.uk/news/9104/irish-ban-on-priority-places-at-catholic-primary-schools

[148] https://www.irishtimes.com/business/economy/income-inequality-in-ireland-relatively-unchanged-since-crash-1.2880569

[149] https://www.maynoothuniversity.ie/sites/default/files/assets/document/O%27Connor%20NatTASCreport_0.pdf

[150] https://www.gov.uk/income-tax-rates

[151] https://www.irishtimes.com/business/personal-finance/ireland-v-the-rest-of-the-world-do-we-pay-too-much-tax-1.3230432

[152] https://www.professionaladviser.com/professional-adviser/news/3026443/uk-state-pension-least-generous-in-the-developed-world

[153] https://www.socialjustice.ie/content/policy-issues/refundable-tax-credits-are-key-dealing-issue-low-pay

[154] http://www.catholicherald.co.uk/issues/catholic-herald-app-2018-06-22/will-irelands-catholic-hospitals-defy-varadkar/

[155] https://www.irishexaminer.com/ireland/the-illusion-of-power-151017.html

[156] https://www.independent.co.uk/news/people/ian-paisleys-most-caustic-quotes-catholics-breed-like-rabbits-and-multiply-like-vermin-9729672.html

[157] https://www.telegraph.co.uk/news/2018/08/24/catholic-church-dominant-society-says-irish-prime-minister/

[158] https://www.nerinstitute.net/download/pdf/qeo_first_edition_2018_finalcomp.pdf

[159] https://www.pivotalppf.org/cmsfiles/Publications/Moving-forward-report—web-version.pdf

[160] https://ec.europa.eu/health/sites/health/files/state/docs/chp_ir_english.pdf

[161] https://www.bbc.co.uk/news/uk-northern-ireland-47955980

[162] https://media.samaritans.org/documents/SamaritansSuicideStatsReport_2019_Dec19_compressed.pdf

[163] https://webarchive.oireachtas.ie/parliament/media/committees/futureofhealthcare/oireachtas-committee-on-the-future-of-healthcare-slaintecare-report-300517.pdf

[164] https://ec.europa.eu/health/sites/health/files/state/docs/chp_ir_english.pdf

[165] https://www.nerinstitute.net/download/pdf/qeo_first_edition_2018_finalcomp.pdf

[166] 'Election is first really big political test for SláinteCare', Irish Times, 4 February, 2020

[167] https://www.thejournal.ie/consultants-pay-slaintecare-4940338-Dec2019/

[168] https://www.irishexaminer.com/breakingnews/ireland/minister-believes-slaintecare-reforms-will-be-completed-before-2030-972849.html

[169] https://www.cso.ie/en/releasesandpublications/ep/p-cp8iter/p8iter/p8rrc/

[170] https://www.cso.ie/en/releasesandpublications/ep/p-cp8iter/p8iter/p8rrc/

[171] https://www.cso.ie/en/releasesandpublications/ep/p-cp8iter/p8iter/

[172] https://www.independent.ie/life/irish-protestants-in-2017-far-from-the-stereotypically-aloof-rich-anglophiles—35621422.html

[173] https://www.cso.ie/en/media/csoie/releasespublications/documents/population/2017/Chapter_5_Diversity.pdf

[174] https://www.cso.ie/en/media/csoie/releasespublications/documents/population/2017/Chapter_5_Diversity.pdf

[175] https://en.wikipedia.org/wiki/Douglas_Hyde

[176] https://www.newsletter.co.uk/news/opinion/ireland-is-a-post-catholic-republic-1-7015913

[177] Interview with author

[178] https://researchbriefings.parliament.uk/ResearchBriefing/Summary/SN04033#fullreport

[179] https://assets.publishing.service.gov.uk/government/uploads/system/uploads/attachment_data/file/847025/CRA_2019_-_main_text.pdf

[180] https://assets.publishing.service.gov.uk/government/uploads/system/uploads/attachment_data/file/856998/2020-01-08_a_new_decade__a_new_approach.pdf

[181] https://assets.publishing.service.gov.uk/government/uploads/system/uploads/attachment_data/file/853118/Disaggregated_tax_and_NICs_receipts_-_methodological_note.pdf

[182] https://www.nerinstitute.net/blog/2015/11/06/the-fiscal-implications-of-irish-unity/

[183] https://www.nerinstitute.net/blog/2015/11/06/the-fiscal-implications-of-irish-unity/

[184] https://ideas.repec.org/p/tcd/tcduee/tep0619.html

[185] https://www.newsletter.co.uk/news/politics/cost-of-united-ireland-would-be-heavy-for-north-and-south-tcd-economists-warn-1-9075364

[186] Gunther Thumann was senior economist at the German desk for the International Monetary Fund during German reunification

[187] https://senatormarkdaly.org/released-research-report-with-senior-economist-at-the-german-desk-of-the-international-monetary-fund-imf-during-german-reunification-showing-northern-ireland-has-near-balance-budget-in-unification-s/

[188] http://www.cso.ie/px/pxeirestat/Statire/SelectVarVal/Define.asp?maintable=EHQ10&PLanguage=0

[189] https://www.nisra.gov.uk/sites/nisra.gov.uk/files/publications/hY5t1a_20174_Publication%20Document.pdf

[190] https://www.nisra.gov.uk/statistics/labour-market-and-social-welfare/annual-survey-hours-and-earnings

[191] https://www.ippr.org/files/2018-03/1521809277_leaving-the-eu-briefing-part2.pdf

[192] https://yougov.co.uk/topics/politics/articles-reports/2019/06/18/most-conservative-members-would-see-party-destroye

[193] https://www.telegraph.co.uk/comment/9717537/Kelvin-MacKenzie-overtaxed-South-needs-its-own-party.html

[194] https://researchbriefings.parliament.uk/ResearchBriefing/Summary/SN04033

[195] https://www.cso.ie/en/statistics/governmentaccounts/governmentincomeandexpenditurea/

[196] http://budget.gov.ie/Budgets/2020/Documents/Budget/Budget%202020_Economic%20and%20Fiscal%20Outlook_B.pdf

[197] https://www.sinnfein.ie/files/2016/Towards-a-United-Ireland.pdf

[198] https://www.nicva.org/article/calculating-public-spending-and-revenue-northern-ireland

[199] Naomi Long, in interview with the author

[200] https://www.instituteforgovernment.org.uk/charts/tax-revenue-capita-england-scotland-wales-and-northern-ireland-199900-201516

[201] file:///C:/Users/Paul/Downloads/46120_b69c7b9d662841619f3e4f85273df2e7.pdf

[202] https://www.oecd.org/tax/beps/

[203] https://www.cso.ie/en/releasesandpublications/er/pme/populationandmigrationestimatesapril2019/

[204] Naomi Long, in interview with author

[205] https://www.pivotalppf.org/cmsfiles/Publications/Moving-forward-report—web-version.pdf

[206] https://www.nisra.gov.uk/system/files/statistics/labour-market-report-january-2020.PDF

[207] https://www.ons.gov.uk/employmentandlabourmarket/peopleinwork/employmentandemployeetypes/bulletins/employmentintheuk/january2020

[208] https://www.nisra.gov.uk/system/files/statistics/labour-market-report-january-2020.PDF

[209] Matt Whittaker, deputy director of Resolution Foundation, tweets dated 29 August, 2018

[210] https://www.nisra.gov.uk/news/labour-force-survey-working-and-workless-households-ni-october-december-2018

[211] https://www.ons.gov.uk/employmentandlabourmarket/peopleinwork/employmentandemployeetypes/bulletins/workingandworklesshouseholds/julytoseptember2019

[212] https://www.irishtimes.com/business/economy/sustaining-northern-standard-of-living-is-a-costly-exercise-1.2597861

[213] https://www.belfasttelegraph.co.uk/business/northern-ireland/weve-yet-to-see-the-full-economic-potential-of-the-1998-agreement-36789890.html

[214] In interview with author

[215] https://ec.europa.eu/eurostat/statistics-explained/index.php/GDP_at_regional_level

[216] http://appsso.eurostat.ec.europa.eu/nui/show.do?query=BOOKMARK_DS-513634_QID_4F7314C9_UID_-3F171EB0&layout=TIME,C,X,0;GEO,L,Y,0;UNIT,L,Z,0;INDICATORS,C,Z,1;&zSelection=DS-513634INDICATORS,OBS_FLAG;DS-513634UNIT,PPS_HAB_EU;&ra

[217] https://www.irishtimes.com/opinion/seamus-mallon-irish-unity-by-numbers-won-t-work-1.3894930

[218] https://sluggerotoole.com/2019/01/27/eastwood-those-of-us-who-believe-in-a-new-ireland-need-to-offer-a-credible-and-positive-vision-we-will-not-protest-our-way-into-one/

219

[220] Fianna Fáil manifesto 2020

[221] https://www.bbc.co.uk/news/uk-northern-ireland-45391529

[222] http://www.competitiveness.ie/Publications/2019/Cost%20of%20Doing%20Business%202019%20Report.pdf

[223] https://www.belfasttelegraph.co.uk/news/northern-ireland/uvf-flags-in-belfast-mixed-housing-scheme-absolutely-appalling-38267969.html

[224] https://www.independent.ie/irish-news/cross-border-operation-launched-to-tackle-fish-poachers-in-tyrone-38379616.html

[225] https://www.ulster.ac.uk/__data/assets/pdf_file/0017/205451/Bill-of-Rights-NI-Draft-Model-Bill-June-2017.pdf

[226] https://www.ark.ac.uk/nilt/2018/

[227] https://medium.com/@ecklewchuk/desouza-case-summary-and-timeline-9deb6fb17402

[228] https://www.irishtimes.com/opinion/assembly-on-irish-unity-risks-being-a-echo-chamber-1.4074327

[229] https://sluggerotoole.com/2019/11/08/citizens-assembly-on-united-ireland-needs-evidence-from-two-sides-and-a-representative-jury-and-consensus/

[230] https://eamonnmallie.com/2019/06/sharing-the-island-a-way-forward-by-professor-colin-harvey/

[231] https://www.youtube.com/watch?v=qKTjrGwWCAA&feature=youtu.be